3-19-63 (62-14536) Traynham
11-11-63

THE GRAND DESIGN

Books by Joseph Kraft

THE GRAND DESIGN

THE STRUGGLE FOR ALGERIA

The Grand Design

FROM COMMON MARKET

TO ATLANTIC PARTNERSHIP

by Joseph Kraft

HARPER & BROTHERS   PUBLISHERS

NEW YORK

In Memoriam
D.H.K.
He understood that in
this world the work of
God is done by the
labors of men.

Contents

Argument

The Grand Design is a synthesis, not a plot. The book seeks to put into coherent pattern many different things being done by many different governments. It could not have been written without the kind cooperation of officials in the Kennedy Administration, and to a certain extent it reflects their views. But there is no presumption to speak for what must surely be the most articulate regime in American history.

In structure, the book is simple. Chapter 1 describes the genesis of Atlantic Partnership, not simply as an idea, but as a working principle of policy. Chapter 2 sets out the international implications of Atlantic Partnership, stressing the spill-over effect of European integration as it touches the industrialized and the underdeveloped nations. Chapter 3 sets out the implications for the United States. Here, a guide to the argument seems appropriate, for some of the concepts are unfamiliar, while some of the terminology is original. The starting point is the view that this country's foreign commitments have outpaced its domestic development. The domestic lag is ascribed to a brake on new social legislation applied almost continuously since 1938 by what in effect constitutes a "negative majority." The negative majority is sustained by a wide variety of economically potent, and numerically large, interest groups which have one thing in common: they have been, or are on the point of being, outmoded by technological advance and are therefore opposed to change. In resisting change, they have an exceedingly useful medium in the subsidy system, which has become a pervasive part of the domestic political and economic environment. It is argued that because Atlantic Partnership provides a means of undoing, or recasting, the subsidy system, it also tends to dissolve the negative majority, thus opening the gates for the backwater of domestic legislation that is necessary if this country is to meet its responsibilities as a world power.

The book was written under the spell of the European Common Market and its achievements. The aim is to expand horizons of thought in this country, and to point out possibilities for constructive action. If many baffling problems are treated with what must seem to be scant respect for intrinsic difficulty, it is in a spirit enunciated by the architect of the Common Market, Jean Monnet:

> We must not be overimpressed by material problems. They are not very hard to resolve. What counts is to make up our minds to see things in the perspective of building the future, not of preserving the past.

THE GRAND DESIGN

1 / Opening the Road

This is not speculation about some grand design for the future," President Kennedy said when he broached his foreign trade program in a speech to the National Association of Manufacturers on December 6, 1961. Undoubtedly, the President was understating matters in hopes of convincing a business audience his proposals were practical. For there is in the Administration speculation about a Grand Design. It is a design for Atlantic Partnership. If it has not crystallized at the very top, it represents views widely and strongly held in parts of the White House, the State and Defense departments, and the Congress. It is likely to mark, along with the Marshall Plan and NATO, another spectacular leap in this country's remarkable transit from isolation to international engagement.

Exactly what new structural forms will emerge is

not yet certain. No more is it clear precisely what steps lie ahead. In the progress from idea to institution, there must be a knitting of bone to bone, and a breathing in of life: organic growth. What is clear, and what is new, is that the Kennedy Administration has found—in foreign trade policy—a functional means for setting the process in motion. It is also clear that the process will go across the board. Besides economic harmony, it will involve more military and political cooperation.

Undoubtedly, the birth pangs will be severe. *"Il faut reculer pour mieux sauter,"* the French say: "You have to step backward, the better to jump forward." For this country the backward step may be as painful as the liquidation of empire has been for Britain and France. It means renunciation of the myth that there is an American patent on supremacy in world affairs. But the sacrifice of illusion, as much as any other sacrifice, brings immense opportunities. Atlantic Partnership will confront the Soviet bloc with a force such as the world has never known. It—and perhaps it alone—will be of a scale to cope with the tasks of developing the Southern continents. And the process of creation is likely to yield for this country some surprising benefits: a shaking of the economy that will sweep aside structural obstacles to much faster growth; a clearing of the political air that will blow away the negative majorities and frustrated ideologies of the recent past. For what is emerging is a unifying intellectual principle for the New Frontier. It is a way to get the country moving again; a means of fulfilling the historic mission of the Kennedy Administration, which is the squaring of domestic affairs with the requirements of world leadership thrust upon the United States in the aftermath of World War II.

II

When that war began, there were eight great powers; when it ended, only one. Germany, Japan, France and Italy had been defeated and occupied. Britain had only just survived. China, in similar condition, was rent by civil war. Though victorious, and with its troops spilling over Eastern Europe, Russia, literally decimated, was on the point of exhaustion. The U.S., by contrast, had upped national income by half, spread its forces across the globe, and acquired a monopoly on a decisive strategic weapon. It attained, in the afterglow of near-universal disaster, an eminence far in excess of its relative strength in population and resources, and there was born the myth of the American Century. The predictable recovery of the rest of the world, however, has made it the shortest hundred years in history. Largely illusory to begin with, this country's seemingly assured predominance has been called into question by an overwhelming problem, a challenge direct and a friendly rivalry.

The overwhelming problem, of course, is the problem of the underdeveloped countries. What they seek is the establishment of modern nation-states with roughly the American standard of living. What they lack sounds like a litany of the damned: they lack capital; they lack skills; they lack energy and other resources; they lack political forms, social structures, administrative routines, well-demarcated frontiers and homogeneous populations. (Every India has a Goa and every Congo a Katanga.) No man can tell how the gap will be closed. How much, for instance, does Latin America need? But there is taking place a total transformation on a universal scale. It will affect three continents engrossing half of the world's land surface and more than half of its population. It will demand transfers of capital that make the present flow look a pittance. It will last this century and beyond. Moreover, in the non-Marxian sense at least, the process of change will almost certainly be revolutionary. Wherever underdeveloped countries have begun to assert themselves, there is apparent a moralistic tone in foreign affairs, and in domestic politics a motif of good guy against bad guy, rich against poor, weak against strong, innocent against corrupt. For the political equivalent of development is convulsion, a turn of the wheel leading to rule by the oppressed. Whether that turbulent process can be held within peaceful bounds—as it has been so far—is very doubtful. It is in any case clear that the United States cannot manage the process alone. Cuba, a speck of sand on a wide strand, affords an example of the grief that comes from trying.

The challenge direct, of course, comes from the Soviet Union. Since the war, Russia has steadily made the kind of progress implicit in a large and rapidly growing population, abundant natural resources and a highly centralized government prepared to manipulate men and resources ruthlessly in the interests of national power. While Russia's gross national product is today only a little better than half that of this country, its rate of growth is more than double: 7 percent against 3 percent over the past decade, according to most reliable estimates. By 1975, Soviet national product will be about three-quarters of this country's. Even that measure is deceptive, for thanks to centralized control and lower consumer expectations, the Soviets channel a far larger portion of their wealth to the turbines of national strength. Probably twice as large a share of national product goes into defense. For investment in new enterprise they set aside more than 25 percent of gross national product, as against less than 20 percent for the United States. They already have better than 10 percent more trained scientists and engineers than this country and are graduating every year more than three-quarters again as many as this country turns out. Certainly, in some key areas—notably space—the Russians have outpaced this country.

Nor can it be assumed that Soviet economic strength rests on starving the consumer; while consumption levels are undoubtedly low, over the past five years the annual per capita improvement seems to compare favorably with consumption growth in the United States. The repeated pledge to "overtake and surpass" the United States is no idle boast. As Abram Bergson writes in his monumental study of Soviet income, "Khrushchev's plans for the future may often be overoptimistic, but they have a basis in fact." With that basis in fact, the Russians have been able to hold together an extensive bloc, and to mount steadily increasing pressures against the most conspicuous hangovers from the era of American supremacy: West Berlin and the strongly pro-Western (not to say client) regimes of Southeast Asia.

The friendly rivalry comes, of course, from Western Europe. Not only has the Continent recovered, but it has enjoyed a heady boom. There was a German miracle, then a French miracle, now an Italian miracle which promises to wipe out within five years one of the world's chronic unemployment problems. The sign and agent of the comeback has been the European Economic Community, or Common Market, now joining six West European nations, but soon to include probably another ten, Britain among them.* Together they will comprise, not a dozen or so tails wagged by a big American dog, but an independent force of undoubted potency. They will have a population (256 million) larger than that of Russia or the United States; a steel capacity below this country's but higher than Russia's; a rate of growth higher than this country's and only a shade below Russia's. They will comprise, by far, the world's fastest-growing market for consumer goods.

European growth, to be sure, has not been directed against the United States, but it has nevertheless posed problems. European goods have displaced American wares not only in parts of Europe and "third markets," but to some extent in this country too. In partial consequence this country has experienced a balance-of-payments crisis, symbolized by European accumulation of dollar holdings, and a gold drain, mainly caused by European conversion of dollar holdings into gold. Balance-of-payments difficulties have, in their turn, sharpened American pleas that Europe shoulder a larger part of the burden of defending the free world, and helping the underdeveloped one. And Europeans who counted it the height of ambition to achieve a "third

---

* The charter members of the European Community are Belgium, France, Italy, Luxembourg, the Netherlands and West Germany. Besides Britain, those likely to join include Austria, Denmark, Greece, Ireland, Portugal, Spain, Sweden, Switzerland and Turkey.

force" now speak of themselves as the "first force."

The collision of these three sets of developments has produced, since 1957, a nearly universal malaise in this country. The nation had been true to its best principles. It had virtually wiped out poverty at home. It had followed peaceful policies in the world, and in some cases made unparalleled peacetime sacrifices for the benefit of other peoples. But the result was not the unbought ease of life. It was sputnik and the U-2 incident and Berlin; it was the balance-of-payments crisis and the small European car; it was Castro in Cuba and a lack of sympathetic approval almost everywhere else in the Southern continents. And it gave rise in this country to a discouragement with the apparatus of politics and an ill-concealed wish for some forceful expression of authority: the "program" of the radical right.

III

The Grand Design is grand precisely because it gives promise of dealing with all these problems. Its essence is creative harmony between the United States and Europe for economic, military and political purposes. It would bring together in a working Atlantic Partnership two separate but equal entities. On the one hand would be this country with its special ties to Canada, Latin America and the Pacific, notably Japan. On the other would be Western Europe with its special ties in

Africa and the Dominions of the Commonwealth. Between them, the two entities would command the overwhelming majority of the world's technical skills, financial resources, consuming power and productive capacity. By cooperative arrangement, the two partners would first adjust mutual differences; and then, while combining forces to hold Communist aggression in check, apply their manifold strengths to the harmonious development of the Southern continents.

Thinking along these lines has been going on for years in various bureaus of the State Department and Pentagon, in the Congress and the White House, and in the nest of universities and semiprivate agencies that serve so often as intellectual pacemakers for the government. NATO, as early as 1949, carried the seeds of Atlantic Partnership, but at that time the European countries were too weak, and too uncertain about the German problem, to hold up an end by themselves. Making Europe strong enough to share the burdens was a cardinal principle of American foreign policy, begun in the Marshall Plan, which stipulated as a prime condition that Europe move toward unity, and continued ever since. Though other issues—Korea, Indochina, Berlin, for instance—came to dominate the news, the notion of Atlantic Partnership hung on, notably among those who watched close up the progressive revival and unification of Europe.

These included practically everyone of eminence in the making of foreign policy over the past fifteen years. Secretary of State Dean Acheson headed the list during the Truman years, but along with him were Under Secretary for Economic Affairs Will Clayton; Senator J. William Fulbright; the European chief of the Marshall Plan mission, W. Averell Harriman; the Ambassador in Paris, David Bruce; the High Commissioner in Germany, John McCloy. Secretary Christian Herter headed the list in the Eisenhower Administrations, but his views were shared by Under Secretary Douglas Dillon, and by the chief of the Policy Planning Council, Robert Bowie. By the time the Kennedy Administration came to office, some of these men were out of public life. But not all. Fulbright was head of the powerful Senate Foreign Relations Committee. Douglas Dillon had become Secretary of the Treasury. Bowie took on a job as a consultant to Secretary Dean Rusk. While Dean Acheson stayed out, the New Frontier fairly crawled with his disciples and associates. Among others, the editor of his speeches, McGeorge Bundy, became the President's special adviser on National Security Affairs; his Policy Planning Counselor, Paul Nitze, went to the Pentagon as Assistant Secretary for International Security Affairs.

To that list of familiar names, the Kennedy Administration added one central figure: George Ball, named Under Secretary of State for Economic Affairs in Janu-

ary, 1961, and the Under Secretary, replacing Chester
Bowles, in November of that year. Ball had been for
fifteen years the Washington representative of the
European unity movement and its principal leader—
Jean Monnet.* As a task-force master in the Kennedy
campaign Ball had presided over comprehensive surveys of American trade, aid and balance-of-payments
problems. He brought with him into hs office three
gifted State Department career men—Robert Schaetzel,†
Stanley Cleveland and Arthur Hartman—all of them
long versed in the European story. Most important of
all, from the very outset, Ball moved to pry controlling
influence over foreign economic policy from an agency
traditionally known for protectionist sentiment—the
Department of Commerce.

Under the Eisenhower Administration, control had
been vested in an interdepartmental committee, chaired
by the Secretary of Commerce. Under the Kennedy
Administration's organizational principle of straight lines
of authority running from the White House to the re-
sponsible department, control should theoretically have
passed from the interdepartmental committee to the

---

* It is said that on first looking over his spacious suite of State Department offices, Mr. Ball remarked, "Monnet isn't everything." Because
his rise in the second year of the Kennedy Administration has been as
dramatic as that of the Secretary of Defense in the first year, it has also
been said that Ball is the " '62 McNamara."

† Mr. Schaetzel was named Deputy Assistant Secretary of State with
responsibility for Atlantic affairs in March, 1962.

State Department. But Commerce balked at that sug-
gestion. Ball then proposed, and Commerce accepted,
the appointment of a coordinating office in the White
House. Commerce balked again when Ball proposed as
head of the office a well-known economist, long identi-
fied with the State Department. It was then agreed that
both departments should submit lists of candidates to
the White House. By a backstage understanding matters were arranged so that one name—and only one
name—would appear on both lists. It was the name of
Howard Petersen, a vigorous Wall Street lawyer, turned
Philadelphia banker, who was known politically as a
fund-raiser in the first Eisenhower campaign, and who
had acquired familiarity with the Common Market
through work in the Committee for Economic Development. Petersen was duly appointed a Presidential adviser. In with him as deputy went a Ball associate—Myer
Rashish, a chief aide on the task-force studies, and for-
merly staff director of Representative Hale Boggs's Foreign Trade Subcommittee.

Long before these events, the revival of Europe and
the balance-of-payments crisis in this country had
prompted certain *ad hoc* approaches toward partnership.
In the economic field, in 1959, Douglas Dillon had proposed to turn the European agency for receiving American aid into an Office of Economic Cooperation and

Development, linking European representatives with those from Canada and the United States. In the military field, in 1960, Secretary Herter had proposed that if the European NATO countries could get together on strategic and tactical questions, a nuclear deterrent, in the form of the Polaris submarine, might be put at the disposition of NATO.

Both these leads were energetically followed in the Kennedy Administration. Backed by Under Secretary Ball and Dillon, the OECD treaty went through the Congress in 1961. A high-level interdepartmental committee to study NATO was set up under Dean Acheson, including Nitze, Bowie, and Henry Owen from the Policy Planning Council. Technically the committee wound up its work with a report (confirming the Herter proposals but adding important safeguards against diffusion of nuclear weapons) in May, 1961. But informal discussions continued. In one talk between Bowie and Owen at the Department in September, 1961—the idea of Atlantic Partnership emerged clearly. Owen arranged for Bowie to outline his views at two high-level State Department-White House meetings. Among those included were McGeorge Bundy, the President's assistant for National Security Affairs; his deputy and later Policy Planning chief, Walt Rostow from the White House; and Schaetzel and Cleveland from Ball's office.

The meetings were held on October 13 and October 17. The Atlantic idea, accordingly, was explicitly in the air.

Still these were merely ideas, bold but naked. Unfortified by anything but the vaguest general interest, they lacked also a mechanism for getting into motion, a means of political engagement. As it happened, there was thrown up in the fall of 1961 a starting mechanism deeply engaging private interest. It emerged from developments in the European Economic Community.

IV

"Europe has taken for me the value of a country," Metternich wrote in 1824 to Wellington, who did not understand. The Common Market is a little like that. The expression of a mystique, and heavily endowed with supranational features, it goes beyond mere analysis. It denotes invisible bonds of kinship, ties that make for what has rightly been called (by Walter Hallstein, President of the European Commission) "membership in the great European family." But the Common Market also has some obvious visible features.

It was set up by the Rome treaty of March 25, 1957, among the European Six: France, Italy, West Germany and the Benelux countries. It provides for the gradual leveling of virtually all barriers to the free flow of men, goods and money among member states. Thus under Common Market arrangements, the Volkswagen concern in West Germany can sell its cars duty-free on the French market—and everywhere else within the Community. By the same token, Renault in France has a free crack at the German automobile buyer and his fellows elsewhere in the Community. But while fostering free trade among member states, the Rome treaty also provides for a Common External Tariff which all member states must apply against goods from the outside. Made up of the average of the old tariffs of the individul states, the Common External Tariff lowers some duties while raising others. Automobile tires from the outside world will eventually have to go against an 18 percent tariff applying to all Common Market countries. That is lower than the former Italian tariff, 28 percent; but higher than the old West German duty, which was zero. Though the emphasis is on industry, the Rome treaty also extends the Common Market principle to "agriculture and trade in agricultural commodities." Specifically, the treaty provides that there be agreement on a Common Agricultural Policy, fixing levels at which European farmers would be subsidized, and to which barriers against foreign agriculture would be raised. Though the emphasis is on Europe, the treaty also provides that former French and Belgian colonies in Africa might avail themselves of Common Market privileges as Associated States.

Inevitably, the very existence of the Common External Tariff has enormous impact on outside states. On the one hand it is almost bound to do injury to nonmembers. The tire manufacturer who shipped wares duty-free to West Germany obviously suffers when, under the new arrangement, he has to pay an 18 percent duty; particularly as his French competitor, being inside the Common Market, can continue to sell tires in West Germany without a tariff. Even in selling in Italy, where the duty comes down from 28 to 18 percent, the outside manufacturer is at a disadvantage; for there too his French competitor sells duty-free. On the other hand, the Common Market countries represent the world's second-richest and fastest-growing market—notably for consumer goods, agricultural products and basic commodities. For those outside countries who wish access to these rich selling opportunities, the Common Market is prepared to make two kinds of accommodations. It will accept new members, providing they subscribe to the Community's principles; or it will negotiate reciprocal tariff concessions.

The pull-and-push effect of the Common Market was markedly evident in the long tug of war with Britain. At the outset, British membership seemed to be excluded by traditional insularity, and the system of preferences for Commonwealth products which ran athwart Europe's Common External Tariff. Britain, however, must export to live—and particularly to the Common Market countries, which take 15 percent of her products. Prime Minister Macmillan, moreover, is not known as MacWonder for nothing. Apparently he came early to the conclusion that Britain would have to join the Common Market. He also apparently decided to exhaust all other possibilities, until the need to get a foot inside the Common Market came home to British producers, thus building public pressure for entry to Europe.

The Macmillan government first tried in direct negotiations with Common Market officials to win tariff concessions without yielding sovereignty or Commonwealth preference. These talks collapsed in March, 1959. Then Britain, in November, 1959, formed the European Free Trade Association (EFTA, or Outer Seven) with six other European nations outside the Common Market: Austria, Denmark, Norway, Portugal, Sweden and Switzerland. EFTA provided for gradual reductions of tariff barriers among member states while allowing each to maintain tariff schedules as it wished against the outside world. EFTA also was a device for putting the squeeze on West Germany, which sends over a quarter of its manufactured exports to the countries in the EFTA group. The theory in some minds was that West Germany, fearful of losing EFTA markets, would put pressure on its Common Market partners to make tariff concessions.

The riposte of the Common Market was to crowd on more sail. On May 12, 1960, it announced a decision to accelerate the schedule for elimination of all tariffs among members and for application of the Common External Tariff to the outside world. The decision had the effect of offering to West Germany immediate replacement inside the Common Market for export sales lost in EFTA. In going along, West Germany threw in decisively with the European Community. Britain was not slow to draw conclusions. Within a matter of weeks a meeting between de Gaulle and Macmillan opened the path that led to Britain's announcement, on July 31, 1961, that she would seek membership in the European Community. The pull of export markets, in short, had won over the Commonwealth, and over Englishry itself.

With Britain (and the other EFTA countries) entering the fold, the American number came up. To be sure, this country, with a broad and relatively prosperous home market absorbing 95 percent of domestic production, was under only limited immediate pressure for export outlets. Distance from Europe—not to mention the Constitution—ruled out any early prospect of American affiliation with the Common Market. So did American commercial ties with Japan and Latin America. As the President put it, speaking at least for those in government: "I have not heard proposed that the

United States should become a member of the Common Market."

Still, this country had some manifestly important interests to work out with the Common Market. For one thing the U.S. wanted assurances the External Tariff would not exclude agricultural commodities—many of them in surplus here—from the growing European markets for grains, meat and tobacco. For another, the U.S. wanted to block any big hikes in industrial tariffs—the more so as balance-of-payments problems and sluggish American demand have suggested the future need of wider foreign markets. Third, it had a very big stake in trying to safeguard the export interests of Latin America and Japan against discrimination by the Common Market. All these claims it raised in August, 1961, at the appropriate international forum—GATT (the General Agreement on Trade and Tariffs), which sits in almost continuous session in Geneva. When the United States presented its claims, the Common Market negotiators, while reserving their stand on agriculture and exports from Latin America and Japan, countered with an offer to reduce industrial tariffs across the board by 20 percent. What, they in effect asked the American negotiators, did the U.S. have to offer in return?

It was, to put in mildly, an embarrassing question. The Reciprocal Trade Agreements Act, which governs American policy on concessions, has been renewed successively since 1934; but since 1951 with increasing restrictions: among them the peril-point and escape-clause procedures, inhibiting concessions that threaten "injury" to domestic industry. In 1958, the Act had been renewed for four years, with terms so restrictive as to leave the American negotiators at Geneva virtually noth-ing to trade against the Common Market offer of a 20 percent cut. Where the Europeans were proffering across-the-board terms, the Americans had to offer their terms item by item.* On at least one item (automobiles) the American offer was contemptuously dismissed by the Europeans as "worthless." By mid-September, the Geneva talks were running into the ground. It was clear that unless the United States was able to hold out promise of substantial revisions in the Trade Agreements Act, the GATT conference would collapse. The issue was up to Washington.

v

Inside the Administration, two groups had been prepar-ing for renewal of the Trade Agreements Act. One was the office of Under Secretary Ball in the State Depart-ment. The other was the special White House office headed by Howard Petersen. While basically in agree-ment on long-range objective, the two groups had con-

---

* It is a mark of the difficulty involved in drawing up an item-by-item list that it took this country two years, from June, 1958, to June, 1960, just to sort out the items on which it might make offers.

centrated on different problems, and at the outset varied in their tactical approach.

The Ball group had focused on foreign relations. It favored a radical revision of the Trade Agreements Act, with authority for the President to deal on an across-the-board basis, and to make very deep cuts. But it was concerned lest precipitate American action in 1962 complicate the entry of Britain into the Common Market. To gain time, it favored letting the 1958 Trade Act expire, and then writing a new bill for submission to a new Congress in 1963. The Petersen group had focused on pushing the trade bill by Congress. Sensing that protectionist sentiment was on the rise, and feeling matters might get out of hand if another year lapsed, it favored renewal of the Act in 1962. As a concession to Congressional opinion, it proposed retention of some of the Act's restrictive features, including peril-point procedures.

Between these two positions, during the month of October, there took place behind the scenes a complex bureaucratic debate. On both sides there was give and take, an articulation of points left shadowy, and in some instances a reversal of position. The upshot was reinforced harmony on principle, and a double knockout on tactical details. Against the Ball proposal for waiting a year, it was effectively argued that, in allowing the Act to lapse, the Administration would lose the initiative. Against the Petersen proposal for renewal with limited changes, it was effectively argued that the President needed far more authority. After hearing both proposals and criticisms, the President bought the boldest features of each plan. He decided to move in 1962, as recommended by Petersen, while seeking major revision, as recommended by Ball. But with both sets of recommended concessions cut away, the Trade Act proposals were politically naked. "For this one," a White House adviser said, "we need more than the League of Women Voters."

At that point the stage was set for the Grand Design. On the one hand, Atlantic Partnership held out the kind of broad, general appeal necessary to push renewal of the Trade Act through the Congress. On the other, the Act was a means of dropping Atlantic Partnership into the hopper of interest politics. In the last week of October, by a process difficult to trace but familiar in government, the logic of the merger suddenly asserted itself. In many minds, in many places, the Trade Act was fused with Atlantic Partnership. The merger expressed itself in a sustained, and many-sided, stretch drive to put Atlantic Partnership across.

Internationally, the decks were cleared for action. After a bitter struggle, the European Six finally agreed on the terms of a Common Agricultural Policy—thus passing the last point of no return on the way to fulfill-

ment of the Rome treaty.* Negotiations on British entry
into the Community were formally opened. In a quick
trip to Brussels early in January, Howard Petersen tied
up the GATT negotiations which had been suspended
in the fall. For its part the United States wrung the last
drop of bargaining authority out of the 1958 bill. The
Europeans, in anticipation of a new trade program,
gave more than they got. Under the final agreement
the United States won tariff concessions on goods that
accounted for $1.6 billion of American exports in 1960;
it granted concessions on items that accounted for $1.2
billion of Common Market exports in 1960.

On the political front, there was under way a discreet
effort to win over, or at least neutralize, a potentially
powerful opponent—the textile industry. The industry
was threatened by serious injury in the event of lower
tariffs. Because Republican votes could not be depended

---

* The Rome Treaty provides that full realization of its objectives be
accomplished over a twelve-year period that is broken down into three
stages of four years each. As the treaty went into effect on January 1,
1958, the first stage ended on January 1, 1962; the second stage will end
on January 1, 1966; the third stage on January 1, 1970. Tariff dismantle-
ment among the members is geared to the stages: 30 percent in the first
stage; 30 percent in the second stage; the rest in the third stage. (In
practice, liberalization has proceeded much faster, and all tariffs among the
Six will almost certainly be eliminated by 1966.) Equally geared to the
stages is a process whereby member nations lose individual veto power
over decisions of the Community, and are brought to accept majority
rule. The French government refused to pass from Stage One into
Stage Two until there had been prior agreement on the Common
Agricultural Policy. In fact, agreement was reached only on January 12,
1962, but the treaty schedule was maintained by the fiction (borrowed
from French parliamentary practice) of, literally, stopping the clock
in the room where matters were being thrashed out.

upon, and because of its strong grip on the Southern Democratic votes, the industry was in a crucial position to gum the works. As a sweetener there had been arranged during the summer an agreement with Japan and Hong Kong, limiting their textile imports to the United States for a year. In addition, the State Department negotiated a world textile agreement, lasting five years, spreading the burden of accepting Oriental imports to the West European countries, and limiting the annual increase in imports received by this country to 5 percent. The Treasury Department announced more liberal write-offs in the tax regulations governing amortization of textile machinery. The White House asked the Tariff Commission to consider a plea by the textile industry for an equalization fee, or additional tariff on cotton goods entering this country.

Inside the Administration meanwhile, there was sustained effort to hold all agencies, and especially the Commerce Department, in line behind a broad, new trade bill. To thrash out agreement on every feature of the bill, there was established a steering committee, headed by Howard Petersen, and including top representatives from all interested agencies: Ball from State; Secretary Luther Hodges from Commerce; Under Secretary Willard Wirtz from Labor; Special Counsel Theodore Sorensen and Deputy Special Counsel Myer Feldman from the White House. In the course of meetings through December, 1961, and early January, 1962, virtually every major issue—including peril point and the timing of the measure—was reopened and then buttoned down. Working hand in glove with the steering committee was a legislative drafting group, put together with an eye to excluding drafters of past bills who might give the Congressional veterans of tariff fights a toe hold on the new bill. It was headed by one of the Administration's best legal minds—the State Department's Legal Adviser, Abram Chayes—and included another—Assistant Attorney General Nicholas Katzenbach* of the Justice Department. It is a mark of the momentum generated inside the Administration that probably the best drafter of all proved to be the man from Commerce—Professor Bayless Manning of the Yale Law School, an old friend of both Chayes and Katzenbach, and a complete stranger to protectionist sentiment, who had been taken on by Commerce for the occasion as a special consultant.

Lastly, there was conducted a concerted campaign of public enlightenment. Under Secretary Ball kicked off on November 1 in a speech to the Foreign Trade Convention in New York entitled "Threshold of a New Trading World." Next day Messrs. Herter and Clayton emphasized the need to take a "new giant step" in a

---

* Mr. Katzenbach succeeded Byron White as Deputy Attorney General when Mr. White was named to the Supreme Court.

report to the Boggs subcommittee. There followed, in serried succession, five more reports to the subcommittee, and then special subcommittee hearings featuring, besides Herter and Clayton, Dean Acheson and a host of prominent economists and businessmen. By that time Secretaries Rusk, Dillon, Hodges and Arthur Goldberg of Labor had all put out statements favoring a new approach to trade, and speeches in the same vein had been delivered by McGeorge Bundy and Walt Rostow of the White House staff. The President took over in major statements to the NAM in New York on December 6, and to the AFL-CIO, meeting in Miami on December 7. The trade bill figured prominently in his State of the Union Message. On January 25, against that sedulously prepared background, he sent to the Congress recommendations for the Trade Expansion Act of 1962.

The covering message was generously sprinkled with expressions of sweep and grandeur. It spoke of "a new chapter in the evolution of the Atlantic Community" and of "the greatest opportunity since the Marshall Plan." It made reference to Western Europe as "a partner . . . strong enough to share with us the responsibilities and initiatives of the free world." To the end of knitting together that partnership, the Administration bill provided the President with authority, over a five-year period, to:

1. Reduce existing tariffs by 50 percent in bargaining on a reciprocal basis with any other country.

2. Eliminate entirely tariffs on products in which this country and the Common Market conducted 80 percent of the world trade. Thus there could be absolutely free trade in those items (largely manufactured goods) which are mainly produced in either the United States or Europe, and where the two partners compete with each other. On goods where even a small tariff can make a big difference, it would be possible to reduce the duty to zero.

3. Reduce or eliminate all tariffs against agricultural commodities produced by the underdeveloped countries of the Southern continents, provided the Common Market countries made similar concessions to the underdeveloped world.

4. Deal in across-the-board terms ("layer by layer") rather than on an item basis ("brick by brick") in lowering tariff walls.

5. Establish an Adjustment Assistance Program providing retraining opportunities and unemployment and relocation allowances for workers and farmers made jobless by tariff cuts; and also providing tax benefits, loans and technical advice to firms injured by tariff changes and showing a disposition to enter new business activity. Adjustment Assistance, in effect, replaced the old peril-point and escape clause provisions which tended to restrict tariff cuts if they did injury to workers or firms.

With the submission of the Trade Expansion Act, the first phase in the formulation of a new American policy came to a close. A map of the world and its troubles had been set before the Congress and the American people. Down the middle was traced the high road the

Administration wanted to travel—the road from Common Market to Atlantic Partnership. At the end of the road, and all along the way, there were evident prospects for profound change in foreign and domestic conditions.

2 / The Prospect Abroad

Backward the course of empire takes its way. Equality —the leveling of superiorities among men—is the universal "wind of change" in domestic affairs, and its natural projection is "self-determination"—the leveling of superiorities among states. Strategic considerations only complement the political forces. Thanks to the new missiles, not even the superpowers will for very long be able to guarantee the security of other states without themselves risking destruction. The spectacle that presents itself in consequence is that of the dislocation of power blocs, the break-up of spheres of influence, the decay of pan-isms. Once bipolar, the diplomatic field is now fragmented.

To this process all countries have had to adjust. The Communist camp has passed from "monolithic unity" to "polycentrism." Britain and France are ending the long-drawn-out, losing battle to hold colonies. The United States has moved from the all-or-nothing anti-Communism of "massive retaliation" to a position apt to command wider political support abroad. In the Congo it has ceased to back the anti-Communist, but otherwise despicable regime of Moise Tshombe. In Laos it has eased support for the anti-Communist, but otherwise dubious government of Prince Boun Oum. By accepting to do nothing about the Berlin wall,* it has once and for all severed connections with those who would use the city as a mecca for discontent, a spearhead of unification and liberation.

From the Western point of view, two dangers attend the adjustment process. One is the familiar danger of Communist penetration. Polycentric they may be, even mellowed, but given an opening the Communist leaders stay not on the order of their entry. Serious men, not only the Radical Right, must be concerned lest the Communists mistake adjustment for weakness, and thus become emboldened to believe they can inflict decisive humiliation on the West. Thus it has been necessary to

---

* It has been suggested that the Administration had no choice in the matter of the wall, if only because it would have taken too long to coordinate plans with Britain and France for retaliatory action to be effective. That may be, though the trans-Atlantic telephone argues a certain skepticism as to how slow coordination had to be. Even so the fact is that not retaliating fitted exactly the logic of the Administration position. It averted two possible dangers that the Administration, rightly, had much in mind: the danger of an uprising in East Germany; and the danger that instead of negotiating with Russia on Berlin, the West would find itself dealing with the East German regime—a truly pretty pickle.

accompany every policy move with signs of unmistakable strength. The political switch in the Congo was underwritten by a United Nations presence. The change in Laos went hand in hand with new determination to hold the line in South Vietnam. Acceptance of the wall was accompanied by a massive call-up of American troops, and by unflagging defense of Western access routes on the ground and in the air.

The second danger is less familiar. It is the danger that the Western countries will emerge from the uninspiring process of retrenchment, disgusted and frustrated; that they will then, in the manner of Spain after empire vanished, turn inward, withdrawing to well-prepared separate shells—Fortress America, Little England, *La France Seule;* that they will abandon even the negative unity forged under Soviet pressure; that they will thus wash their hands of effective responsibility for the rest of the world. Here lies the real danger to those who would remain free, to the poorer countries of the Southern continents, and to the United Nations and all other international cooperation.

It is against that deadly prospect that Atlantic Partnership asserts itself on the international scene. It is a means of assuring, as the President put it at his news conference of February 8, 1962, that the Western countries will "not turn in, but rather out." It provides constructive purpose at a time of seeming regression. It directs the Western powers to the tasks of perfecting their own cooperation, of resisting Communist aggression through NATO, and of building the Southern continents. It is a new principle of association in a period of disassociation, a force for positive unity, a powerful base for the assertion of mastery over drift.

II

The British physicist P. M. S. Blackett once observed that where state policies affecting masses of people were concerned the only good ideas tended to be simple ideas. Atlantic Partnership is simple to the point of being obvious. At its core is one of the world's most prominent geographic features—the mighty ocean highway. It rests on cultural traditions stretching back twenty-five centuries to ancient Greece, and currently expressed in a general similarity of language, religion and mores that heads up in a common sense of values. Like political institutions—parliaments, parties, bureaucracies, judiciaries and executive offices—link most of the members. So does an ineluctable push toward urban industrialism and its institutions: corporations, unions, science and the welfare state. To these ingrained, almost unconscious bonds, there is added the acquired habit of deliberate consultation in dozens of different cooperative organizations. "Eurocrats"—the superb civil servants who man the central institutions of the Common Market, and who embody a harmony transcending national differences—already exist in most of the industrial countries of the free world.

No doubt these ties will be severely tested in the early stages of Atlantic Partnership. Bitter memories lie behind (only some of them connected with colonialism's long day's dying) and predictable difficulties loom ahead. Britain must be ushered into the European Community, with arrangements made for her Commonwealth and EFTA partners. A special form of membership will probably have to be worked out for the European neutrals—Switzerland, Sweden, Austria. Even if the President's Trade Expansion Act goes through, there will be hard bargaining among Americans and Europeans on mutual concessions—particularly as they apply to Japan and Latin America. While the European Community's Common Agricultural Policy has been agreed upon in principle, details are vague—notably as regards price levels. It is becoming increasingly clear that before details can be spelled out, there will first have to be worked up a common policy embracing, at least, all temperate-zone food products.

Still, there have recently been striking signs of effective collaboration. In the fall of 1961, at the first formal meeting of the Organization for Economic Cooperation and Development (OECD), the member nations took an unprecedented pledge of joint effort toward a principal economic goal: "the attainment during the decade 1960 to 1970 of a growth of 50 percent in the gross national product of the 20 member countries taken together." In two world textile agreements, the major European countries joined the United States in agreeing to share the burden of admitting slowly rising quotas of textiles from the cheap producers—Japan, Hong Kong and India. Through OECD and NATO, there have been remarkable cooperative efforts to meet the American (and British) balance-of-payments problem. Ten countries, including Japan, have joined the United States in making available to the International Monetary Fund a reserve of $6 billion to be used in preventing runs on the dollar or pound. To the same end American financial authorities have been working in the exchange markets with their French, British, Italian and German opposite numbers to hold down disturbing variations in national interest rates. Agreements have also been worked out whereby American dollar spending for troops in France and West Germany is matched by French and West German purchases of arms in the United States. By these means, the United States has been, through 1961 at least, able to meet its balance-of-payments problem without taking deflationary steps in the domestic economy.

Further projects for cooperation among the industrialized free nations abound. Common Market circles buzz with talk of a single European currency that would take much of the pressure off the dollar. Equally, there is talk of a joint commodity strategy that would both coordinate (by agreed stipulation on what items had military value) Western sales to the Communist bloc in the interests of security, and protect (by agreed standards of fair trading practice) against the increasingly acute problem of Communist dumping on Western markets. There are rich possibilities for increasing the flow of trans-Atlantic tourism—and in a two-way direction. Even on that most intractable of problems —agriculture—there have been important stirrings.

At present, a study of the House Agriculture Committee shows, more than eighty nations use subsidies, controls, export premiums and other devices to help their farmers. High-cost, inefficient producers (some of them in Western Europe, still plowing with oxen) are kept in business, while the efficient producers (mainly in the United States, Canada and Australia, but also in parts of France, Denmark and Holland) accumulate surpluses. The tendency, as one government official has pointed out, has been to "regard agriculture as a ceremonial institution, like the Beefeaters and ravens at the Tower of London, to be maintained at national expense. Only the Beefeaters and ravens at least attract tourist income, which redundant farmers do not."

A first dent in that prevailing condition was made through the Common Agricultural Policy agreement reached by the European Six in January, 1962. While details remain to be worked out, it is clear that the European champs—the farmers of France—have landed several blows on the European stumblebums—the farmers of West Germany. Prices will be supported somewhere between the relatively low French costs and the extremely high West German costs. Moreover, in the course of negotiating on Britain's admission, the Six have had to face up to the problem of two really low-cost grain producers—Britain's Commonwealth partners, Canada and Australia. One very promising scheme was put forward by the Dutch Minister of Agriculture, Sicco Mansholt. "The idea," in the striking phrase of the London *Economist*, was that "the present mess of national support schemes might eventually be shunted off" to an international cartel representing producer and consumer interests. The cartel would buy up commodities at a fixed, low price—low enough so that in time the most inefficient producers would be driven out of the market. It would sell, also at low prices, to consuming countries. Such surplus as existed would be channeled on a systematic basis to the underdeveloped countries short on foodstuffs. A fund, put up by the producer countries, would help farmers forced off their lands, and also countries—notably Britain—facing steeper food prices. Thus, at one stroke, there would be met the headaches of agricultural protection, of high-cost, marginal producers, of surpluses and of feeding the underdeveloped countries.

The Mansholt Plan is a long way from adoption; indeed, it has, at least temporarily, been rejected. But it is a gauge of what may be possible. Together with the textile agreements, and the various actions on balance of payments, it suggests the rich opportunities in cooperation among the advanced nations of the free world. In these circumstances, the indications are that the first, difficult period preceding Atlantic Partnership can be safely traversed. If so, the Atlantic nations will be able to turn their attention to two problems of the exterior—meeting the Soviet threat through NATO, and building the underdeveloped world.

III

Cheers were in order when the NATO alliance passed its tenth birthday back in March, 1959. The alliance had held together through an exceedingly difficult decade. It had absorbed the shock of Korea and Indochina. It had weathered a new republic in France, a government with Communist members in Iceland, and political change in every other member state. It had taken in two East European members (Greece and Turkey) and navigated safely the tricky shoals of West German rearmament. Under all these pressures it had not yielded a square inch of territory to Communist encroachment; on the contrary, one European state—Austria—had emerged from occupation. Still, the official birthday toasts were sober, while the unofficial ones were positively melancholy. "The Western alliance is in serious danger," Henry Kissinger wrote in the *New York Times*. *Le Monde* said: "*Il y a donc une malaise atlantique.*"

The Atlantic malaise has since deepened, with the alliance giving off louder and louder signals of distress. British and French nuclear programs have whetted a German thirst that threatens, in the words of one European agency, "nuclear anarchy." Conventional force levels, minimal to begin with, have never been met; both British and French armies in Europe are well under strength, while the American force is "a quartermaster army." Central NATO machinery is in disarray. "NATO ministers," former Secretary Herter recently observed, "meet at relatively long intervals, usually in an atmosphere of semicrisis, and then go back to their national preoccupations. In the meantime, the North Atlantic [permanent] Council meets under conditions somewhat remote from the central power issues of the world." On two issues that are NATO business if anything is—the German question and disarmament—the alliance has had nothing useful to contribute, except for General Norstad's *cri de coeur*, "We must stand to arms." On both issues, in consequence, the tendency has been to by-pass the alliance.

What is common to all these troubles is a grave discrepancy between the strategic outlook of the United States and that of its principal European allies. In general, British, French and German thinking is fixed where the United States stood about four years ago —on the doctrine of "massive retaliation." All three countries tend to regard large nuclear weapons as indispensable, and where once they feared the United States might be trigger-happy, they now are apprehensive lest the American finger freeze on the trigger. "You say that you would risk your own destruction to save Europe," a French journalist told Stewart Alsop. "But we don't believe it—we can't." In that spirit, Britain has built a nuclear deterrent as the centerpiece of its defense force. France is following suit. The indications that West Germany is moving in the same direction are now unambiguous. At the December, 1961, NATO ministerial meeting, Defense Minister Franz Josef Strauss asked for a NATO nuclear deterrent that would have a German finger very close to the trigger. A month earlier he told a Georgetown audience that "Possession of nuclear weapons, and control over these weapons, is becoming the symbol, and even the characteristic aspect, of the decisive criterion of sovereignty."

Hand in hand with the nuclear emphasis there goes,

as it did in this country, a de-emphasis on conventional forces; the theory being that added firepower changes, in *Le Monde*'s phrase, "the question of manpower." Britain's decision to build a nuclear force, in 1957, was accompanied by the end of the draft, and a whittling down of troops in Europe by a quarter. France moved to become a nuclear power at precisely the time almost her whole army was tied up in Algeria and current French plans call for a manpower cut from 750,000 to 450,000 men. While West Germany has been obliged to raise conventional forces as an entrance fee to the NATO club, the drift of Bonn's thinking is very clear. Colonel Gerd Schmückle, Defense Minister Strauss's press chief, has referred to building conventional forces at a time of nuclear supremacy as "military alchemy."* "Do you think," a West German man in the *strasse* with two nephews in the *Bundeswehr* asked a *New York Times* reporter, "they're going to stand and fight with rifles against the Russian atom bombs?"

Intransigence on negotiations with the Soviet Union is equally part of the "massive retaliation" syndrome. "Massive retaliation" rests on the proposition that if all is risked, anything can be held; the logical corollary is that if anything is yielded, all is lost. In the past few years, the French and Germans have followed this logic

---

* His exact words were: "Die Idee vom konventionellen Krieg in Europa ist militärische Alchimie."

to the bitter end. They have repeatedly protested against negotiations on disarmament and on Berlin. Indeed, General de Gaulle, in his speech of February 5, 1962, boasted that:

> By taking the stand of refusing to negotiate on Berlin . . . we have spared our allies and ourselves catastrophic withdrawal.

In sharp contrast to the Europeans, Washington has moved far from the all-or-nothing principles of "massive retaliation." The moving spirit of American strategic thought emphasizes the need to create a maximum number of alternatives between all and nothing. "Our objective now," the President said in his first Defense Message to the Congress, "is to increase our ability to confine our response to nonnuclear weapons." It is to that end that the Army has been reorganized, and given a rise in manpower and in troop mobility; that the Marine Corps and Special Forces have been expanded, that there has been special stress on the Polaris and Minuteman—both "second-strike" missiles; and that there has been a little noticed, but very important, tightening of Presidential control over commanders disposing of strategic and tactical nuclear weapons. For the same reasons it has seemed sensible to the Kennedy Administration to combine positions of strength with willingness to negotiate on disarmament and Berlin.

Not only does Washington differ with the Europeans; it views their approach with some alarm. It is clear that each new addition to the nuclear club makes room for the next; the problem of curtailing the spread of nuclear weapons, as Albert Wohlstetter has pointed out in a brilliant essay, is less the problem of the Nth country than of the Nth Plus 1 country. It is doubtful that any European nation can put together a true deterrent capability—with not only nuclear weapons, but missiles, warning systems and protected sites. Far from serving as a deterrent to the Soviet Union, the European efforts to acquire individual national nuclear capabilities may act as a temptation for Communist aggression.

It has not been easy for Washington to communicate its views to the European allies. National sensibilities are involved; at least some of the American officers in NATO headquarters have not got "massive retaliation" out of their systems. Still, a brave try has been made. In a speech in May, 1961, in Ottawa, the President indicated this country's belief that the first priority in Europe was for nonnuclear forces. Secretary McNamara reiterated that view in blunter terms at the December, 1961, NATO ministerial meeting. But the plain fact is that the Europeans have not been getting the message.

In part, at least, because they don't want to. General de Gaulle is the last man to yield to exhortation. The

British feel keenly the financial pinch. West German leaders cannot easily accede to what seems like a position of relative inferiority. But there is also another reason for the deaf ear. It lies in the process of strategic thought.

The genesis of useful strategic ideas in the nuclear age is a complex, evolutionary process of inner debate. It requires concentrated immersion in strategic problems, a high level of abstract reasoning, continuous testing of ideas by interchanges between military staffs and scientific people, and repeated adjustments to technological change and political developments. Learning is an essential part of the process. A crude measure of what goes on is provided by the semipublic debate on the uses of tactical nuclear weapons.

Systematic analysis of the possibility began early in 1948 with Project Vista—an assembly of scientists and military men under government auspices at the California Institute of Technology. In early 1953, the U.S. Army announced experiments on the impact of nuclear weapons in battlefield conditions. In 1956, the Army announced activation of a division equipped with nuclear arms. Public explanation of that policy was begun in 1953 in books published by the physicist Ralph Lapp and two professional officers, George Reinhardt and William Kintner. It was continued in a series of magazine articles (by Bernard Brodie in *Foreign Affairs* and

Harper's, by Paul Nitze in *Foreign Affairs*, by Arthur Hadley in the *Reporter*) and reached high tide in 1957 with Henry Kissinger's book, *Nuclear Weapons and Foreign Policy*. In substance all these books and articles, like official Army doctrine, took the view that, as Kissinger put it in 1957:

> Limited nuclear war represents our most effective strategy against nuclear powers or against a major power which is capable of substituting manpower for technology.

By that time, events were already beginning to point in another direction. The development of the hydrogen bomb enormously increased the need to prevent all-out war, and raised the prospect that even tactical nuclear weapons might be in the megaton range. Korea indicated how difficult it was to keep a limited war limited, particularly in view of likely divisions among military leaders. And the possibility of arms control—particularly of a test-ban agreement—tended to compromise the continued testing required to develop tactical nuclear weapons. Accordingly there grew up, inside the military staffs, acute unease about tactical nuclear weapons, and that too found outside expression. In 1957 and 1958 articles by James King (in *Foreign Affairs*), William Kaufmann (in *World Politics*) and Thomas Schelling (in the *Journal of Conflict Resolution*) all concentrated attention on the dangers of "escalation" to all-out nuclear war once tactical nuclear weapons were introduced. In the light of these arguments, strategic thinking began to shift. By 1960, Kissinger was acknowledging that nuclear defense, far from being "the most effective strategy," was the "*last* and not the *only* resort." Official policy reached that conclusion in 1961. It was the fruit, in short, of more than a dozen years of intense, inner debate.

From this strategic planning process the Europeans have been virtually excluded. Themselves without nuclear weapons (except for Britain, which has no delivery system), they have not had to plan nuclear strategies on the national level. In theory, to be sure, they participate at the NATO level. But, as former Secretary Herter has indicated, the ministerial meetings are too infrequent to give constant attention to serious business, while the permanent Council, meeting in Paris, is too remote from the other seats of power. The Standing Group, officially NATO's most prestigious military body, has declined in importance, and is no longer even attended by the chairman of the American staffs. Strategic planning, in these circumstances, has tended to gravitate around the office of the Supreme Allied Commander Europe, SACEUR. Made prestigious by the tenures of Generals Eisenhower, Ridgway, Gruenther and Norstad, and held aloof by not unfamiliar military attitudes toward civilians and security, SACEUR and staff have become a satrapy of the American military. It is secondhand from SACEUR that the Europeans derive their notions of nuclear planning. Hence the lag in their ideas; and hence too, the nearly neurotic fixation on the question of whose finger is on the trigger. For as NATO is currently organized and run, SACEUR is a constant reminder to the Europeans that their destiny lies in an alien hand.

This passing on of ready-made conclusions has indeed characterized the American relation with Europe throughout the post-war era. This country has been well-meaning; it has been understanding; it has been most generous. But the relationship has been imbued with benevolent paternalism. It cannot continue that way—least of all in the military field. The Soviets are on the point of being able to deliver a nuclear attack on the United States—thus inevitably raising European doubts about the American pledge to treat an attack on Europe as an attack on this country. Technology is making possible, and safety is making desirable, the withdrawal of the American deterrent from the Continent, and its relocation in the seas, or the remote parts of the United States: a further fillip to European doubts. Lastly, the Europeans—together if nothing else—are undoubtedly in position to do much more than they have been doing about their own defense. They will act separately from the United States, drifting further and further away, if this country continues to hand down ready-made decisions. But the two Continental entities can act jointly—and as rough equals—in Atlantic Partnership.

A way to meet the NATO problem—and the first step toward Atlantic Partnership in the military field— has been suggested by the British defense writer, Alastair Buchan. It is that allied officials (both civilian and military) be drawn into the American strategic planning process. To that end, the civilian side of NATO would be strongly reinforced: first, by the designation of important political figures from each member country to sit on the permanent Council; next, by the sending of top civil servants to the NATO Secretariat. These organs would then come to do in NATO on a permanent basis what *ad hoc* committees of "Wise Men" have done from time to time. They would not make, but they would force decisions. They would compare the cost of different weapons systems, and their technical and political advantages and disadvantages. They would debate targets and investigate contingencies—for example, what might be done in the event of a squeeze on Berlin. The Europeans would thus exchange concern with the shadowy control of a finger on the trigger for concern with the substantial control of formulating strategic plans. They would, undoubtedly, learn some useful lessons.

Exposure to the disposition of American nuclear power, and to the American command and control system, is apt to lay, for several years, the dangerous myth that major attack on Europe could come without provoking American retaliation. A feel for the cost of nuclear weapons and their associated paraphernalia, plus a grasp of the dangers implicit in diffusion of weapons, can dull the liveliest appetites for an independent nuclear force. Once convinced of the credibility of the American deterrent, and the infeasibility of separate national deterrents, the allies could reasonably be expected to look to their conventional forces. After all, there is, in terms of resources and manpower, no reason why the NATO ground force in Europe should not match that of the Soviet Union. "They look eight feet tall," one Pentagon expert says, "because we act four feet tall."

Useful by itself in a military sense, a European concentration on ground troops would pay an added bonus in slowing down the rush to nuclear weapons. Diplomatically, a stay in the race is of crucial importance. For the time being the elements of accommodation in Europe—the potential background for a Berlin or even a German settlement in the cold war—include the possibility of a mutual limitation on the scale of armaments. To be more specific, Russia might guarantee Western access to Berlin in a new statute; the West might in turn guarantee present frontiers against disruption by force; and the bargain might be sealed by agreement not to maintain nuclear weapons in the European heartland. To be sure, despite their well-advertised fear of Germans bearing nuclear weapons, the Russians may not be willing to accept any such arrangement. Still, there is no reason to write off the possibility of agreement before testing it—at least not just yet; not while American nuclear weapons are still an effective deterrent in Europe, and while allied strategic concepts are so far apart.

In the long run, it may be necessary to create a NATO deterrent—if only to head off the drives toward independent national nuclear capabilities. Many different schemes have been advanced, including one by Mr. Ben Moore, that there be a NATO force of nuclear missiles controlled by the Europeans without an American veto power. In such conditions, it would be no bad thing if the Europeans had first become familiar with the American strategic thought process. It would be a decidedly good thing if the force came into being at a time when the Continental balance included British membership in the European Community, and active American cooperation with it. Indeed, it is only under such conditions that the West can see, whole and steadily, the most awful implications of the German question.

The fact is that Germany faces East as well as West.

The temptation to treat independently with Russia, to repeat the 1922 deal of Rapallo and the 1939 Nazi-Soviet Pact is not some vicious concoction of the Free Democrats, the Ruhr industrialists and a peculiar ambassador in Moscow. Neither is it a mere expression of Germany's division. It is an enduring possibility written on the map of Europe. Competitive bidding for Germany between East and West has been going on since the war, and will continue into the predictable future —even if, in the fullness of time, the Russians come to understand that a united Germany is less of a menace to them than one disunited and discontented. The West cannot win the bidding by pretending it doesn't exist; still less by muttering "Rapallo" whenever a German opens his mouth in Moscow. It can win in the future only as it has won in the past: by making it indisputably preferable, both in terms of welfare and of power, for the Germans to throw in their lot with the Atlantic powers. That means engrossing Germany in the full majesty of the Atlantic vision—in the building of Europe, in the defense of the free world, and in the titanic effort to develop the Southern continents.

IV

On the endless roster that lists the needs of the underdeveloped countries, two items stand out: capital and technology. Together they make up the *sine qua non* of twentieth-century life—the stuff of industry and efficient agriculture, of schools, hospitals, power plants, roads, cities, rising standards of living and the modern welfare state. In relative abundance in the Northern continents, they are in acute short supply throughout the Southern continents. That they can be passed on is suggested—even proved—by the history of the industrial revolution, and its progress from Britain to Europe, North America, Russia and Japan. No doubt there will have to be political and military ties between the advanced countries and the backward ones. But the hope is that they will be minimal. Practically speaking, the problem of the underdeveloped world—the problem of the next half-century—is the problem of transmitting massive doses of capital and technology from the rich countries to the poor countries.

Traditionally, the principal transmission belt has been one so commonplace as to be almost invisible—trade. When Ghana sells cocoa and Nigeria palm oil to Britain; when Brazil sells coffee and Venezuela oil to the United States; when Egypt sells cotton to France, and the Congo copper to Belgium, they become exporting countries, and they receive in return money (that is, capital) with which they can—and generally do—buy machinery and equipment (that is, technology). Even in the first stages of trade, long before transactions become important there is generally some transmission of capital and technology. Britain, besides buying Argentine beef, built the Argentine railroads to move the beef; American companies, besides buying Saudi oil, have built pipe lines, power facilities and sea- and airports in Arabia. In total, some $30 billion annually is involved in trade between the underdeveloped countries and the non-Communist industrial world. This commerce constitutes by far the largest source of capital and technology available to the Southern continents. To a large extent, trade remains what the late Professor Ragar Nurske of Columbia said it was in the nineteenth century: "a means whereby a vigorous process of growth came to be transmitted from the center to the outlying areas of the world."

As an engine of spreading growth, however, the classic pattern of exchanging primary commodities against capital goods has some obvious shortcomings. There may be little substance in the notion (very popular among leaders of the newer countries) that to be an exporter of primary materials and an importer of manufactured goods is somehow *infra dig*—a shameful badge of colonial status. By that reckoning the United States (which exports wheat and imports typewriters) and Russia (which exports oil and imports machine tools) would be colonies. But it is true that raw material prices fluctuate far more violently than the prices of manufactured goods: cocoa, for instance, dipped in

price by more than half in a sixteen-month period in
1954-55; the new nations, as one of Mr. Kennedy's
task forces has pointed out, "are losing more in income
as a result of cyclical movement of raw material prices
than they receive through economic assistance." It is
also true that proceeds from the sale of primary commodities tend to stick to the fingers of a particular class
—the cotton pashas of Egypt, for example, or the sugar
barons of Cuba. Not only does such concentration exclude the broad masses from a share in trade, but it
often creates commercial oligarchies prone to support
corrupt and reactionary regimes—that of Farouk in
Egypt, for example, or of Batista in Cuba.

Worst of all, the pattern of exchanging primary
goods for capital and technology is based on special
conditions. It derives from the nineteenth-century experience of Britain and the outlying "white man's lands"
of North America and Oceania. It presumes that the
underdeveloped countries will have abundant land
(making possible cheap agriculture and mineral exploitation) and a sparse population (consuming only a small
portion of the produce). That pattern still applies in
most of Africa, and for parts of Asia, the Middle East
and Latin America. But in the most important part of
the underdeveloped world—in India, Pakistan, Egypt,
Algeria, Mexico, Brazil, Argentina—the trade pattern
comes to grief in the population explosion. In all these

countries contact with the industrialized world through trade has brought medical knowledge and basic sanitation, and, in consequence, a population boom. Because of population pressure, land has become dear, prices of agricultural commodities have risen, and the local population has come to consume much of the produce. Even though very large, moreover, export trade in primary products has not created nearly enough employment to absorb the rapidly growing population. In these countries economic growth barely keeps pace with population growth—and sometimes lags behind. The result is a declining standard of living—the so-called "immiserization" of trade.

To offset some of the obvious failures of the trade pattern, foreign aid, the *wunderkind* of the postwar era, has been brought into the picture. By direct grants and loans, the richer countries make capital available to the governments of the poor countries—not to special classes, and not only to those countries endowed with raw material surplus. Technical assistance brings the skills of advanced culture directly to the fields of the poorest peasant. Military aid, in part at least, makes available for investment government funds that would otherwise have gone to defense. Gifts of agricultural surplus, though justly criticized on many grounds, can also be important; applied in conjunction with public works projects as partial pay for the workers, the food can even be made to work as capital.

Still, it is clear that foreign aid, too, has serious weaknesses. If only because of the customary asymmetry of the partners, bilateral dealing—the United States with Guatemala, say, or France with Gabon—subjects aid programs to acute political strain. Much of the promise of technical assistance has been eroded because, at least in this country, the pay necessary to recruit talent invites a style of living bound to cause resentment abroad; what makes the American seem ugly in Saigon is doing what comes naturally in Philadelphia. Aid through agricultural surplus tends to be very spotty; it is, indeed, dependent on what is left over from commercial transactions. Most important of all, the level of aid is much too low. While a heavy amount of not very educated guessing is necessarily involved in the calculations, a number of independent estimates (one by a team of United Nations experts; another by an MIT research team under Walt Rostow and Max Millikin; a third by a University of Chicago research group) indicate that the underdeveloped countries could usefully absorb $8 to $9 billion annually in economic assistance. At present the Western contribution is running at about $4 to $5 billion. Lastly, it cannot be too much emphasized that aid is necessarily a junior partner to trade. As the

GATT ministerial conference observed at its November, 1961, session:

> Although international aid is now and will continue to be essential . . . aid can be no substitute for trade. In the final analysis, economic development will be paid for from the earnings of the countries concerned.

The combined shortcomings of Western aid and trade programs have left in the underdeveloped world an important void for Communist entry. Communist success, indeed, seems to depend almost exclusively on Western failure. To date anyhow, the Communists have ranged along the margin of the field, darting in occasionally to make spectacular plays, but never fully participating. The Communist bloc nations bought cotton from Egypt, rice from Burma, rubber from Indonesia at times when they were in glut on Western markets. They bought Guinea's bananas when France wasn't having any, and Cuba's sugar when the United States barred the door. Similarly, their major aid projects are the Bhilai steel mill in India and the Aswan dam in Egypt, both proposals previously rejected by Western countries as an uneconomic use of scarce resources. The most notable features of their aid programs—low interest rates, long duration, quick and easy negotiations—seem specially designed to show off to advantage against

Western, and notably American, practice.

It is, of course, true, that the Communists claim, and that many believe, that centralized state control over the economy is the most efficient way to promote rapid development. But even that claim seems to find its takers in special countries—Egypt, for instance, and Cuba—that is, in precisely those areas where trade patterns fostered a rich oligarchy working hand in glove with a corrupt regime. The Communist pattern, in other words, seems useful less to organize development than to beat down interest groups that get in the way of development. Such groups are not universal, and experience suggests that, peasantries apart, they collapse rapidly. As to the peasantries, the Western way is, by Khrushchev's own recent account, far superior to that of the Communists, and properly presented could pay great dividends.

No doubt, Communist programs of trade and aid in the Southern continents will expand. Present levels—about $500 million annually—are ridiculously small, given the size and resources of the bloc. Internal growth plus changing taste patterns are apt to stimulate a rapidly rising Communist demand for the products of the Southern continents—notably tropical agriculture. At the same time, the bloc should have available increasingly large surpluses of capital, machinery and skilled technical personnel. In the next decade, the Communist countries are apt to pass from a thorn in the flesh, which they are now, to a major competitor in the Southern continents.

It is a competition the world can well afford. Not only does it raise the total amount flowing from rich to poor, but it provides a stimulus for bold venture; after Bhilai, the Western countries also began building steel mills in India. No more than the West are the Communists immune from shortcomings in their trade and aid programs. Cement they sent to Burma had set before it was unloaded; their technicians at Aswan are not loved by the Egyptians. Far from priming new nations for Communism, economic relations with the bloc seem to put them specially on guard. An impressive list of countries—Egypt, Guinea, Burma, India, Syria, Iraq—have accepted Communist economic help only to harden their political stand against Communist penetration. Moreover, the West will not stand still. Atlantic Partnership holds out the prospect of major improvement in economic programs for development of the Southern continents.

The chief change would be a pooling of effort through an expansion of the Development Assistance Group of the Organization for Economic Cooperation and Development (OECD). Membership, now confined to the industrialized countries of the non-Communist world, including Japan, would be enlarged to permit permanent representation of the African, Asian and Latin-American worlds. To the organization there could then be appended, as Miss Barbara Ward has pointed out, any number of *ad hoc* institutions— "banks, development funds, trade groups, common markets, statistical services, and, above all, common policy-making organs." There would thus be in existence a permanent forum, linking rich countries and poor ones, and concentrating on problems of economic development.

In the aid field, the industrialized members of OECD are already on their way to setting a general, national quota for annual contributions. The figure most commonly used as 1 percent of Gross National Product, set aside each year by each state for aid to the underdeveloped countries. The quota system would lead to an immediate increase of non Communist aid by nearly 100 percent to $10 billion annually. Assuming, as pledged in the first OECD meeting, general growth in the free world economy, the system would also assure a rising level of aid. It would, to boot, bring into the aid business a number of countries—among them West Germany, Italy and Japan, which have not hitherto shouldered a fair portion of the aid burden. While there seems to be little hope of skirting the annual Congressional appropriations process, a target, and especially a target being met by other nations, would ease con-

siderably the annual defense of the aid program to hos-
tile legislators; the program might, in that way, also be
shielded from the gusts of transitory events.

Pooling would almost certainly improve the quality
of technical assistance. To the large financial resources
of the big states, there would be added the wealth of
technical talent—willing to serve abroad under onerous
conditions, and gifted in languages—that is to be found
in the smaller states. Danes, Israelis, Swedes, Swiss and
Norwegians would, in effect, act as aid proxy for the industrial giants that have so little rapport with the new
countries. Distribution of aid would, no doubt, stir intense bickering among the recipients; there was, after
all, bickering among the European beneficiaries of Marshall Plan aid. But there are worse things than for officials
of the new countries to become acquainted—even in-
timately involved—with the problem of dividing scarce
resources among many claimants. The multinational con-
text, at least, would provide insulation against the suspicion of discrimination that arises under the lopsided
conditions of direct bilateral dealing between the powerful and the weak. Indeed, the requirement that aid programs have the support of many countries, both on the
giving and receiving ends, is likely to foster the development of neutral, business-like principles as criteria for
determining levels of assistance. Aid would come to be
withheld or extended, as it now is by such institutions

as the World Bank, on grounds that are above suspicion. A barrier would be started against those would-be Machiavellis—abundant in the foreign ministries, defense establishments and intelligence services of all countries—who seek to give aid for favors, or to elicit it by blackmail.

In the trade field, far larger benefits are possible. President Kennedy's Trade Expansion Act, which initiates Atlantic Partnership, foreshadows one of the benefits explicitly. It points the way toward eventual abolition of all discriminatory barriers raised by the industrial countries against the primary products of the Southern continents. This would involve a scaling down of tariffs on tropical agricultural products; a moderation of revenue taxes, by which many countries, especially on the Continent, hold down consumption of tobacco, coffee, cocoa and tea; a dismantling of quota systems by which most advanced countries restrict imports of cane sugar, and by which this country checks imports of oil, lead and zinc.

Along with an increase in the volume of trade in primary products, Atlantic Partnership holds out promise for stabilizing commodity prices. Striking a fair balance between the conflicting interests of a multiplicity of suppliers and a multiplicity of buyers is anything but easy. Still, a very large portion of the world's traders will find representation in the economic organs serving Atlantic Partnership. There will be no question of control over the lion's share of the market. And tools for stabilization by international accord are at hand. One of these is the buffer stock system currently in effect in the International Tin Agreement. Under this system participating countries set up an international management, and endow it with independent resources. When the world price of a commodity falls, the international manager buys, building up a buffer stock. When the price rises, sales are made from the stock. In that way the most violent fluctuations—the deepest troughs and highest peaks in price—tend to be smoothed out.

Another possible system is the multilateral long-range contract, currently in effect in the International Wheat Agreement. Under this scheme, each exporting country (a) agrees to provide a certain quota of the commodity at a fixed maximum price and (b) retains the right to sell the same amount of the commodity at a fixed minimum price. Each importing country (a) agrees to purchase a certain quota of the commodity at a price not lower than the minimum and (b) retains the right to buy the same amount at a price not higher than the maximum. The aggregate of export quotas equals the aggregate of import quotas. Each exporter has a price floor beneath his quota; each importer has a price ceiling over his quota. A certain amount of stability is thus assured.

The provision of more aid, and of more commodity trade at stable prices, should go a long way toward smoothing the road for the sparsely populated countries of the Southern continents. There remains, however, the crucial, agonizing question of the large, heavily populated countries, many of them already midway to development. On these the population problem alone imposes the imperative of industrialization. In no other way can they find employment for their teeming millions. It is already clear that these countries will concentrate, initially at least, on the light, processing industries—textiles, shoes, glass, toys and other simple manufactures. The countries concerned have in abundance what such industries most demand—a large supply of unskilled labor. Many also have on hand the necessary raw materials—fibers, wood, leather. The technology required is simple, and easily acquired. The model of Japan, in other words, will be followed—indeed, is being followed—by India, Pakistan, Egypt, Algeria, Mexico, Brazil and the Argentine.

Across their path, however, lie two, not disconnected obstacles. Even workers turning out textiles and shoes must be fed, and the backward, low-yield peasants of the new nations are not always able to do the job—not, certainly, as it should be done. In addition, the goods produced—the textiles, shoes, etc.—must be bought. But the local public, composed very largely of these selfsame backward peasants, has only a very limited power to consume. It is to meet these contingencies that "balanced development"—the modernization of agriculture simultaneously with the development of industry—is generally enjoined upon the poor countries by the rich. Just as sensibly were thrift and temperance enjoined upon the poor of England in the early stages of the industrial revolution. And just as vainly. For the modernization of a traditional peasantry, when land and capital are scarce, is not only exceedingly slow, but political explosive. It involves something the Communists, with all their drive, organization and ruthlessness, have never been able to achieve. It means breaking the mold of a primordial force that has successfully been resisting change since the beginning of time.

In the interim—and that means for the next half-century—there is a job cut out for the Atlantic Partnership. Under the Mansholt Plan, or some variation rationalizing temperate zone agriculture, the huge surpluses of grains, meats and dairy products turned out regularly by the advanced countries can be directed in a steady stream to the underfed, industrial masses of the new countries. Under an arrangement like the Textile Agreement, though perhaps more generous, the rich countries can gradually open their own abundant consumer markets to a swelling stream of manufactured goods pouring out of the underdeveloped world. No doubt, acceptance of these imports will force painful contractions on competing industries in the advanced countries. But it is, as a team of GATT experts under Professor Gottfried Haberler recently pointed out:

> a natural and economic development that relatively poor countries with high population densities like India and Hong Kong should export cheap labor-intensive manufactures in order to import foodstuffs like wheat from developed countries such as Australia, Canada and the United States which are rich in land and capital.

What is in the offing, in short, is a complete transformation of world trade patterns. Atlantic Partnership provides a frame for making the changes in an orderly, harmonious fashion; within this frame, burdens too heavy to be borne by any single country can be spread out among many countries. More importantly, Atlantic Partnership provides a ferment which, if only for political reasons, no single country could possibly generate. The dynamic seed is the Common Market, which, in Europe, forced a consideration of problems long neglected. European settlement of these problems in turn forced their consideration by all her trading partners; it is thus that the Mansholt Plan and the Textile Agreement emerge just as Britain prepares to enter Europe and the United States discusses closer ties. The European Idea, in other words, is being exported round the globe. European economic integration has a spill-over effect, touching first the industrial nations of Western Europe; then North America, the "white" Dominions, and Japan; and lastly the underdeveloped countries. In this sense, the Common Market provides a principle of "permanent revolution" for the whole non-Communist world. Its beneficial effects will be felt by poor nations and rich alike—and not least by the richest of all, the United States. For what Atlantic Partnership promises the United States is not only the reinvigoration of the economy but even more the breaking of a political stalemate that has for years held the nation in check.

3 / The Prospect at Home

Dr. New Deal has been replaced by Dr. Win The War." The jocular remark made by Roosevelt in 1943 describes a condition that began five years earlier and lasted nearly twenty years after. Deadlocked on most domestic issues, but ready to support bold venture in foreign affairs, American politics has been fixed in incongruity for nearly a quarter-century.

Domestic affairs have been characterized by an absence of sweeping social legislation. Since the Wages and Hours law of 1938, there has been repeated picking over the corpus of the New Deal, but no major, new legislative departure—not in urban affairs, not in education, not in labor, not in the incidence of taxation, not even in civil rights. The characteristic political form has been stalemate: liberal Democrats in the White House from 1938 through 1952, with a conservative coalition of

Southern Democrats and Republicans controlling the Congress; a Republican in the White House from 1952 to 1960, with the Democrats in control of Congress from 1954 to 1960. While the division has been narrow, events record a clear victory for forces opposed to domestic change. There has been, in effect, a negative majority.

Foreign affairs have been characterized by expansion of commitments at a dizzying pace. American troops have gone, not only to Europe, but to the distant corners of Asia: Korea, the Lebanon, Laos, South Vietnam. Economic aid, begun on an emergency basis to Greece and Turkey, was extended for four years to Western Europe, and then shifted to the underdeveloped countries as a permanent fixture. Treaty commitments first crossed the Atlantic, next spanned the Pacific and then completed the world circuit in the Middle East. Every step of the way, the widening assumption of foreign responsibility found overwhelming support in the Congress. Both parties, in their Presidential candidates, have come out decisively for engagement and against isolation. In foreign affairs there has been, in effect, a positive majority.

For many years the two majorities coexisted without apparent tension, feeding perhaps on the temporary postwar lead enjoyed by the United States over the other powers. But some time in the second term of the

Eisenhower regime, the incongruous harmony was shat-
tered. Almost overnight, in a series of dramatic events,
domestic stalemate came into collision with growing
foreign commitments. By the election of 1960, omens of
troubles were everywhere—as obvious as the moving of
Birnam Wood to Dunsinane. Sputnik had called into
question American education, science and research. The
balance-of-payments crisis had cast a long shadow over
the competitive potency of the domestic economy.
Anti-American sentiments—most vigorously expressed
in precisely the places that had most participated in this
country's largesse and cultural influence—suggested
something wrong with the quality of American life.
A second in the Olympics even raised doubts about the
nation's stamina.

Between these circumstances and the Presidential
election of 1960 there was more than a dim connection.
Youth and undoubted ability, plus a shared capacity for
political engineering, may have convinced some of an
underlying likeness between the two candidates. But
Senator Kennedy made himself the voice and embodi-
ment of determination to match domestic performance
to the requirements of world leadership. "Prestige"—
the sum of national attributes heading up in international
stature—he made a main issue, and "growth." His slo-
gan, "The New Frontier," signaled advance. And over
and over again he reiterated a phrase no ghost ever

wrote, the umbrella phrase of his campaign: "This country has to get moving again."

For Mr. Nixon, in contrast, "experience" was the umbrella phrase. To "growth" he made the response of the cracker-barrel sage: "growthmanship." And over and over again he lapsed from prepared text to nostalgic recollection of the simpler virtues of a simpler past: the brother who wanted a toy train; the brother who wanted a pony; the "little country grocery store."

Though muddied by the Catholic issue and traditional sectional alignments, the choice of the nation was spoken with a clarity rare in national politics. In virtually every way possible the country voted a tie. The popular vote margin was the closest in this century—110 thousand votes out of 68 million. In eleven states (including California, Illinois and Texas), the winner's edge was less than 1 percent. Sectionally there was a stand-off: Kennedy held the deep North and deep South, while Nixon made inroads in both places and took the West. The three border regions were all split: In the East-West border, Ohio and Indiana were for Nixon, Illinois and Michigan for Kennedy; in the North-South border Delaware, Maryland and West Virginia were for Kennedy, Tennessee and Kentucky for Nixon; in the South-West border, Missouri and New Mexico were for Kennedy, Oklahoma for Nixon.

What the tight division expressed was an absence of

consensus—a nonmandate. In the Congressional session which followed, the familiar incongruity returned—not harmoniously but with a vengeance. Emergency changes were voted to help distressed farmers and depressed areas. Foreign aid and the defense budget went through in relatively good shape. But the one piece of domestic legislation apt to work important long-term change— the education bill—was roundly beaten. The negative majority was back in the domestic saddle. American politics had come to an historic turning point—and missed the turn.

Through its entering wedge, the Trade Expansion Act, Atlantic Partnership offers a second chance. The Act makes explicit once again the underlying tension between domestic stagnation and overseas commitments. Against the negative majority in domestic affairs, it brings to bear the positive majority in foreign affairs.

II

Domestic stalemate is a widely recognized malady, generally ascribed to popular apathy and confusion. As remedy, the conventional wisdom prescribes "leadership" and the enlightenment of "public opinion."

Now it is no doubt true that because so many Americans are so well off, the spur of urgent need is out of domestic reform; there is a "hedonism of the *status quo*." It is also true that world events, particularly in their strategic aspects, are more complex than ever before; American destiny is now "unmanifest." "We stand at Armaggedon and do battle for the Lord" was a fit standard for 1912, to which men could repair; its 1962 counterpart would be phrased in the abstract vocabulary of modern strategy (it might go something like: "We stand at Minimax and do battle for the Second Strike") and would be incomprehensible. Still, to prate of "leadership" and "public opinion" is to recommend air-conditioning as a cure for malaria. Complacency and poor understanding are part of a permissive climate favoring inaction. But inaction is not only allowed; it is willed by a negative majority to which great force is imparted by a vast interest group that at once embodies and protects widespread, economic maladjustment.

Maladjustment, of course, is the regular condition of society. Ways of life develop by organic growth, are passed from generation unto generation, and express themselves in routine and habit; in the Anglo-Saxon countries even "the angel of progress moves from precedent to precedent." Between this slowly shifting custom and the demands of a rapidly changing technology there is inevitable cultural lag. Analysis wars against experience in every country, and the means of accommodating the tension supplies a key, perhaps *the* key, question of social organization. In general, the Communist countries, and many of the newer countries, have thrust

upon the national state the dirty job of forcing individual compliance with the requirements of progress. The
free world, in contrast, has accorded large scope to what
Adam Smith called the "invisible hand"; the pushing
around of men has been left to the largely unseen con-
straints of individual needs and opportunities. In the
United States, at least, an unparalleled richness of opportunity combined with a relative absence of established ways to make the system work exceedingly well.
Virtually all analysts came to agree that the distinct
American characteristic was mobility, "ceaseless motion" as Tocqueville called it. "America," Bryce wrote,
"is the land of change."

For a variety of identifiable reasons, however, the "invisible hand" has been less efficacious in the postwar
period. To begin with, the rate of technological change
is setting an ever faster peace. Science may be as old as
Pythagoras, but, as Rutherford used to say, this is its
Elizabethan age. Ninety per cent of the scientists who
ever lived were born in this century; in this country the
number of private research laboratories has doubled in
the past fifteen years, while industrial expenditures on
research, up by 200 percent in the first seven years of
the postwar era, increased by 300 in the next seven years.
But the social impacts of technological change—the
knuckles on the invisible hand, so to speak—have been
softened by a thick webbing of protective arrangements

in the form of quotas, subsidies, tariffs, feather-bedding and administered prices. Though these arrangements are exceedingly costly ($3 billion for farm supports in 1960 alone), the price was easily bearable in the heady years of postwar prosperity. By the time foreign commitments forced a domestic accounting, it was plain that there was being nursed, within the dynamic bustle of the American economy, a large and protected sector of economic laggards: the victims of progress.

Foremost of these is the American farmer. Fertilizers, machinery, cheap electric power, pesticides and the internal combustion engine have made two ears grow in the place of one—and then some. Output of crops per man-hour of work has tripled since 1949. Output of livestock and livestock products per man-hour has risen by nearly 50 percent. The average farm worker now produces enough food and fiber for about thirty persons. A large portion of the farm community has made the most of technological advance. Four percent of all the farms in the country make over $40,000 annually, and yield a quarter of the produce. Nearly a third of all the farms, producing more than 80 percent of the total, return more than $5,000 annually. But the over-all impact of technological advance has been consistent surplus over domestic demand, and a resultant drop in farm prices and total income. Alongside the modern farmers in American agriculture there stands a huge rural poorhouse. Forty-three percent of the farm families in the country have incomes of less than $3,000 annually. Though concentrated in the South among small cotton and tobacco growers, agricultural poverty is far more widespread than generally realized. In 1959, the average cotton farmer in the Southern Piedmont made $654, or 26 cents per hour of work. The average cotton-tobacco farm in North Carolina yielded $1,292. The average dairy farm in eastern Wisconsin returned $853 income to its family owners. The average spring wheat farms in the Northern plains brought in $207. The average sheep farm in the Southwest brought in $463.

Except as victims these rural poor barely participate in the modern economy of the nation. They make up the bottom of the standings in the national averages of health and literacy; many, indeed, are debarred by educational deficiency and physical handicap from migration to industry. In age they average well above the national level. They consume next to nothing; a Department of Agriculture study of a depressed rural area in Kentucky shows a family of four spending, in 1956-57, $176 for all household operations. Even the balm of expectation is denied them, for predictable technological advance makes them increasingly less competitive with the efficient sector of agriculture—a surety, in effect, of a dwindling stake in the future.

Industry, as much as agriculture, harbors a lagging

sector, a vast collection of scattered enterprises victimized by progress. The Department of Commerce (in the September, 1961, "Survey of Current Business") lists over a hundred major products and services showing "declining trends." The use of diesel fuel for locomotives, and of oil and natural gas for heating, has outmoded large sectors of the coal industry—both bituminous and anthracite. Plastics have taken a toll on lumbering and the glass industry. Newer metals have eased demand for steel. Exhaustion of many of the best American lodes and development abroad have made many zinc, copper and lead mines noncompetitive in international markets. Some domestic oil producers are in the same bind. A switch to motor and air transport has cut heavily into passenger and freight traffic on the railroads. Several factors (wages not too far out of line with those paid by the progressive sector of American business, and mechanization in Hong Kong, Japan and India) threaten much of the domestic textile industry—the nation's largest single industrial employer. The same combination has had the same effect on shipping and shipbuilding. And in the prosperity of the past fifteen years the appliance market has become virtually saturated.

The impact of these declining industries shows up to some extent in unemployment statistics. While the national average, in October, 1961, was 6.8 percent, the

average in textiles was 10.9 percent; in mining and for-
estry, 10.4 percent; in transportation equipment, except
for autos, 8.1 percent. But those are only partial measures, for it must be noted that a declining industry usually affects a whole community. A truer index is supplied
by Depressed Areas; scratch a Depressed Area, and there
is uncovered a declining industry. Fall River, Lowell
and New Bedford, Massachusetts, all speak for textiles.
Butte, Montana, is a monument to nonferrous mining.
Altoona, Pennsylvania, tells the railroad story. Youngs-
town, Ohio, is a measure of steel. San Diego, California,
puts the case in shipping and shipbuilding. And West
Virginia—the whole state of West Virginia—indicates
what is happening in coal.

The exact over-all numerical strength of the victims
of progress is not easy to assess—but neither is it small.
Something like ten million people live on marginal
farms. Textiles alone employ over two million workers.
For political purposes, there can be added to these num
bers the socially maladjusted, notably those resisting
racial integration, and the Radical Right.* An important

---

* The Radical Right presents a fascinating political "case." Geographi-
cally it finds its support in the area of the nation's most rapid growth:
the Southern Rim of the country stretching from California to Florida.
Los Angeles County supplies the two Congressmen who are acknowl-
edged members of the John Birch Society: Edgar Hiestand and John
Rousselot. Arizona is the base of Barry Goldwater. Oklahoma provides
headquarters for the Christian Crusade. Texas is the seat of the National
Indignation Convention. These men and movements are chiefly backed
by native whites who have done well—often in economic services—by the
regional upsurge; they are the *rentiers* of progress. And their attributes

booster is also introduced by the overrepresentation of rural as against urban voters in the Congress. The declining interests, in short, comprise a very large fraction of the political nation. Threatened by change, their assets on the wane, they make up the troops of the negative majority. Their vested interest is protection against change.

The very strong laggards can take care of themselves.

---

include the force and self-confidence that typically go with sudden success, and that strike others as manifestations of simple-minded crudity.

Besides personal success, however, growth has brought with it alien conditions. There has been an influx of industry, and of the "newer immigrants": Negroes, Mexicans, Jews. Civil rights has become an issue, and housing, and trade unionism. In urban centers and universities cosmopolitanism rears its head. Cheek by jowl with the districts of Hiestand and Rousselot are the constituencies that sent to the Congress two of its most liberal, not to say radical, members: James Roosevelt and Chet Holifield. While Phoenix remains safely white, Tucson, Arizona's other big town, has many Mexicans. And besides Goldwater, Arizona also supplies the most partisanly liberal member of the Kennedy cabinet: Interior Secretary Stewart Udall.

It is the tension between these two elements of growth that gives force and cutting edge to the Radical Right. A prescriptive movement in a fluid situation, it seeks to reserve to itself, by denying to others, the fruits of progress. A declining interest inside a progressive area, it is in natural harmony with the negative majority; the shared aim is to preserve privilege by staving off change.

The Radical Right concentrates on foreign issues, in part because they are in the air, something it is easy to get people excited about; in part because its true ends cannot gracefully be exposed to public view; and in part out of a shrewd instinct for what is going on. What has induced growth in the Southern Rim, and brought in the influx of new immigrants and new problems is chiefly the defense program, with its camps, bases and concentration of weapons system industry and proving grounds. Indirectly at least, foreign policy has brought tension to the Southern Rim, and in fighting it the paladins of the Radical Right get close to the bone of their troubles. In the long run, it seems likely that the Southern Rim will be inundated by newcomers, and the Radical Right overcome. Until the balance tilts, however, it would be logical for the Radical Right to become increasingly important, and for American politics to become increasingly shrill in partisan tone.

Well-entrenched unions practice feather-bedding galore: the railroad industry, according to one management estimate, pays out half a billion dollars annually for work it doesn't need. Industrial giants, notably in steel, enforce "administered prices." But these are crude exceptions to the rule. The typical pattern in an industry victimized by progress resembles the pattern in farming: a few, large and very efficient producers, swimming in the pond with a swarm of small, less efficient producers. By a curious inversion, the true strength of the strong lies in the weak. The high prices which the small mill owner of the Northeast needs to stay in business represent that much more profit to the textile giants who have moved South. Demands for privileges sound a lot better coming from the mouths of independent oil producers—those sturdy little fellows—than from the mouth of Jersey Standard. Most of all, the strong need the weak to plead effectively for the device that par excellence links declining interest with the negative majority—the subsidy.

That dirty word appears just once in the index to the Federal Budget ("operating-differential subsidies" under "maritime activities," Department of Commerce). But one authoritative study (by the Joint Congressional Economic Committee in 1960) took six pages just to list government subsidies and concluded that "subsidies have expanded to the point where few segments of our economy are completely unaffected by them." Another, more self-serving study (by the House Committee on Agriculture, in 1954) makes the staggering judgment that "The subsidy is the oldest economic principle written into the laws of the United States. . . . There is no officially recognized definition of a subsidy as such, and no unchallengable compilation can be made of the costs of subsidies down through the years." In any case, whatever the cost, whatever the definition and whatever the form, subsidies are legion.

The oil men have their depletion allowances and import quotas. The railroads, built thanks to land grants, now seek, and in some cases get, forgiveness of local taxes on the property. Civil air carriers get extra pay for ferrying the mail. Shipbuilders and operators receive payments to offset lower costs abroad. Zinc and lead interests, once nourished on "defense" stockpiling, are now paid the difference between a "fair" price and the world market price. Producers of cotton, corn, wheat, rice, tobacco and peanuts (the basic commodities), and of oats, barley, grain sorghums, rye, wool, mohair, tung oil, honey, milk, and butter fat (the nonbasic commodities), all receive price supports. The wheat and cotton growers also have an export subsidy, while both beet and cane sugar producers benefit from import quotas. And, of course, the whole system feeds upon itself, and multiplies.

The textile industry currently offers a juicy example

of cumulative subsidization. In consequence of the farm support program, cotton sells in the United States at 8½ cents above the international market price, and quotas bar foreign cotton from this country. To compete on the world market, cotton exporters selling abroad are paid a subsidy. American textile manufacturers, as a result, pay 8½ cents a pound more for cotton (even cotton produced in their own country) than their foreign competitors. To be sure, the textile manufacturers are already helped by tariffs, quota arrangements and special depreciation regulations. But, in addition, they are now asking for an equalization fee, or additional tariff, to offset the 8½-cents-a-pound differential favoring their foreign competitors. It is a case, as the *New York Times* has pointed out, of seeking a "tariff to offset a subsidy that compensates for a price support." But within the terms of the system it is no more than just. For the subsidy system—massive, confused and interlocking—has a force and logic of its own. And if the victims of progress are the troops of the negative majority, its preferred battleground, indeed its principal weapon, is the subsidy system.

By itself the easy availability of subsidies fragments whatever pressure there may be for sweeping change. Even the poorest farmers direct their efforts, not to a new farm program, but to getting a penny more in the support price or an added acre in the allotment to be planted. It is not unfair to say that the Catholic bishops contributed to the defeat of the education bill because they hoped to win a subsidy for their system of private education. Neither is it unfair to say that the Southern Democrats voted against the bill out of fear that a larger federal role would speed school integration. And the alliance of Southern Democrats and Catholic bishops for the defeat of the education bill represents a classic case of the negative majority in action.

Far stronger than the hope of winning new subsidies is the fear that the props and privileges of the system may be swept away—a justified fear, for both political parties, at least implicitly, have developed programs for paring away the most conspicuous of the laggards and the most costly of the subsidies. The Democrats would achieve that end through government programs expanding the public and service side of the economy to the point where massive new job opportunities would lure people from declining enterprises. The Republicans, in contrast, would apply tight credit policies and allow much freer play to market forces. Defending against these threatened assaults has been the chief purpose— and, so far at least, the supreme triumph—of the negative majority. It has been able to play each party off against the other, weakening both in the process. Against the Democrats it has arrayed the conservative Congressional coalition, and successfully mobilized charges of corruption, inflation, bureaucracy, unbalanced budgets and Communists in the State Department—all the anti-government issues that head up in the image of "the mess in Washington." Against the Republicans it has invoked a more subtle tactic—the tactic of splitting tickets to produce divided government.

Farm voting is a case spectacularly in point. Normally Republican, the farmers, to protect their subsidies, supplied the votes that turned what looked like a Dewey landslide into Truman's election in 1948. In 1952 and in 1956, they went for Eisenhower. But in the 1954 Congressional elections, about half the rural counties which had given Eisenhower a majority two years earlier went Democratic, and that pattern repeated itself in 1958. "We need a farm program," one Republican county chairman explained to Samuel Lubell, "and we ought to work on both parties to get it. I'm for Eisenhower, but I'm voting Democratic for the Senate."

The state of Montana provides a concentrated example of the same phenomenon. A land of subsidies, with agriculture the chief interest and mining next, it is also a paradise of divided government. Republican in the Presidential elections of 1952, 1956 and 1960, it has two Democratic Senators (Mike Mansfield and Lee Metcalf) and a House delegation with one Republican (James Battin) and one Democrat (Arnold Olsen). In 1960, the state elected a Republican governor and Democratic lieutenant governor. The state Senate is safely Democratic (38 to 17); the state House safely Republican (53 to 41).

Even more than the hopes it inspires, or the fears it provokes, the subsidy system works for the negative majority by sheer complexity. No one unfamiliar with the system—not Dickens at the top of his form—could possibly imagine the ponderous definitions, the elaborate spelling out of an infinity of possible contingencies, the meticulously detailed statements of eligibility, the marvelously intricate scheduling of rates and payments, that go into a subsidy bill. Here, for the innocent, is a piece of salutary reading—a description (taken from a study by the Joint Economic Committee) of the shipping industry's operating-differential subsidy:

> The operating-differential subsidy is intended to compensate U.S. operators for higher operating costs than those borne by foreign operators. Under title VI, sections 601-603, of the Merchant Marine Act of 1936 (49 Stat. 2001), the Federal Maritime Board is empowered to grant an operating-differential subsidy to aid a citizen of the United States in the operation of a vessel to be used in an essential service, route or line in the foreign commerce of the United States. The operating-differential subsidy, which is intended to place the proposed operations of such vessels on a parity with those of

foreign competitors, is the excess amount of the cost of items of operating expense in which it is found the applicant is at a substantial disadvantage in competition with foreign vessels over the estimated cost of the same items of expense were the vessel operated under registry of a foreign country whose vessels are substantial competitors of the vessels covered by the contract.

The determination of the amount of subsidy due is a complex process. The operating-differential subsidy payments are determined and stated as percentages of the subsidizable expense of a U.S. operator. Separate rates are determined for each type of expense (e.g., wages, subsistence, maintenance and repairs, stores and insurance) for each type of vessel on each trade route which takes into consideration each principal foreign-flag competitor. Calculating these rates requires a large amount of foreign cost information which must be maintained on a current basis. Since many foreign-flag operators are not willing to divulge their costs, which are to be used as a basis for determining subsidy payments to their subsidized U.S.-flag competitors, the Maritime Administration has been compelled to obtain the information elsewhere and as a consequence has been compelled to base at least part of its calculations upon assumptions. . . .

It is in these tangled thickets, in this fetid miasma, that the forces of change regularly stumble, stop and then strangle to death. The Congressional captains of the negative majority—veterans of hearings that stretch back decades, and nitpickers to the core—are in their elements. But the ordinary citizen cannot hope to penetrate the mystery. Presidents and Cabinet ministers recoil in frustration or go along with the game; a Secretary of Agriculture expounding what was supposed to be the government sugar program to a Congressional committee not long ago turned to a representative of the producers on one point to find out "what the drafters really meant." Even experts throw up their hands in despairing surrender. A recent study of American sugar policy (by the Food Research Institute of Stanford University) comes to this dismal conclusion:

> The complex issues involved in sugar policy afford no simple solution but cannot properly be ignored.

Indeed not. For such complexity is the principal nexus between the stagnant elements in the economy and the negative majority which enforces political stalemate. One hand washes the other, and the harmful consequences are well-nigh incalculable. By themselves the laggards do damage enough. They are a standing obstacle to more rapid growth. They place a heavy drain on the public treasury. They are a constant source of inflationary pressure. They work to blight whole regions. They tie up men, money and resources that should be released for more productive work. As the prime supporters of the negative majority, moreover, their pernicious influence is given even wider effect. They present on a massive scale and in high relief a conspicuous example of something for nothing; cushioned by the inefficient, as we have seen, even the efficient are tempted to rest on their oars. They tie up both parties in a stand-off that makes a mockery of the political process. They work to deepen into acute and frustrating misery problems that could be solved—problems of urban life, for instance, and education. They are, in a word, the hard nut that must be cracked before the country can be got moving again on a sustained basis.

But stalemate does not overcome itself. Taken on its own terms, the domestic deadlock can no more be broken than the circle can be squared. A new factor must be brought into the equation. What Herbert Leuthy saw in France, half a dozen years ago, is now true of the United States, to wit:

> that this economic, social and psychological structure, distorted by . . . inflationary development, protectionism, regimentation by economic guilds and cliques, could not shake itself out of its state of ossified equilibrium, but that the shaking would

have to come from outside, and that the lever by which this might be done was the "European Market."

III

The case of the twenty-nine electrical producers convicted of conspiracy to fix prices in February, 1961, was widely taken as evidence of sharp practice in American business. It was at least as much evidence of leaden torpidity. Bad as the knavish ways of the conspirators may have been, they were more than matched by the foolish ways of the patsies—the public utilities which buy electrical equipment. Not once, apparently, did the utilities compare prices to see if they were being had. Not once did they take bids on generating equipment from foreign producers outside the conspiracy. It was the TVA that did that. When the first TVA contracts began going to foreign companies, there came from the domestic producers a cry of "Buy American" such as never before. But there has since ensued a curious thing. By improving manufacturing techniques, the American companies have been able to outbid the foreign competitors in this country. It is widely believed that they can now undersell the foreigners abroad.

For those who would gauge the future under Atlantic Partnership, the case of the electrical producers is full of lessons. It teaches that some of the fear of foreign

competition is exaggerated—not to say deliberately
trumped up. It teaches that there is broad room for improvement in American business. It teaches that under
the spur of competition improvements will be made.
It suggests that what the little dose of competition imported by TVA did for the electrical producers, the
larger dose imported by Atlantic Partnership can do for
the whole economy.

It is, of course, no easy thing to chart the future of
the economy. An accurate guide would require surveys
of millions of different products made by thousands of
different firms under the most widely ranging conditions
of wages, profits, materials costs, technology and business organization. It would equally have to anticipate
the reactions of businessmen, technicians and workers
whose stock in trade is ingenuity—that is, the unortho-
dox reaction. In fact, no man knows precisely what effect Atlantic Partnership will have on the domestic
market.

Even so, it is possible to get a feel. Banks and private
research institutions have studied likely changes in
American trade. The National Industrial Conference
Board has compared costs of selected American enterprises operating here and abroad. Trade statistics covering the period since the beginning of the Common
Market and the Japanese recovery provide useful point-
ers. Some businessmen have expressed their views in testi-

mony to the Congress. From these sources, it is possible
to identify the impact of the freer trade implicit in
Atlantic Partnership on large groups within the American economy.

One large group comprises the stuff on which the
postwar American boom has fed—consumer durables.
Included in this group are all the accoutrements of
modern American living, and most notably home appliances. Abundantly produced and consumed in this
country during the postwar years, but now entering a
period of decelerating domestic demand, these goods
are, in Europe and Japan, just beginning to come into
mass consumption. Here, for example, is an account of
the European selling opportunities for consumer durables given by an executive of the Whirlpool Corporation in recent Congressional testimony (delivered with
Europe divided into the Common Market Six and the
Free Trade Area Seven, it makes use of those catego-
ries):

> If you will examine the chart which is before you,
> you will see why the European Common Market
> excites U.S. manufacturers. In the first column you
> have the figures which show the actual market sat-
> uration here in the United States. Take the first
> one, automobiles. We are already more or less sat-
> urated, 100 percent. But now look at the figure for

the saturation of the "Seven." It is only 25 percent. Look at the figure for the "Six," 19.

Now turn to television sets. Here in the United States, the actual saturation is 89 percent for television sets, but in the "Seven," it is 61, and in the "Six," it is only 10.

Now radio sets—here in the United States, the market is already saturated to the extent of 96 percent, but in the "Outer Seven," it is only 24 percent, and in the "Inner Six," it is only 20.

Let us look at one of the products with which I am most familiar, refrigerators. Here we have a market which is saturated to the extent of 98 percent, whereas in the "Seven," the saturation of the moment is only 14 percent, and in the "Six," it is only 12 percent.

Another product that has a special interest to me, washing machines—in the United States, the market is saturated to the extent of 91 percent, whereas in the "Outer Seven," it is only 23 percent, and in the "Inner Six," it has not even begun, it is only 12 percent.

A second group comprises the wide range of products, manufactured by the more sophisticated and advanced sectors of American business, that find no competitive counterpart abroad. These include electronic systems; construction, communications and conveying equipment; processed food and food machinery; aircraft, both large and small (and notably helicopters); special paper products; new chemicals and drugs. Despite the high speed at which technology crosses frontiers, the large research and investment components in these industries, plus the rapidly rising expectations of the American consumer, suggest that American companies may keep a continuous lead in innovating new products. The story of office equipment machinery in the past decade, as Professor Raymond Vernon of Harvard has noted, is a case in point:

> In 1950 United States exports of cash registers, adding machines and standard typewriters had a commanding position in world markets, while United States imports of these products were insignificant. By 1959 United States producers in these lines were being sorely pressed by foreign competitors. Nevertheless, despite growing pressure in these sectors of their business, United States producers were expanding their position in newer products during the period, enjoying a swift rise in their exports of punch-card equipment, electronic computers, and electric typewriters.

A third large category of business consists of products that Professor Vernon has described in these terms:

> a relatively simple technology, capable of being transmitted across international boundaries . . . [containing] a significant amount of labor-cost content, justifying the search for a location where labor

costs are low; and [having] in its finished form . . .
a relatively high value per pound, thus being able
to absorb international shipping costs without a serious competitive handicap.

Textiles fit pre-eminently into this category, and so do
shoes, toys, plastic articles, gloves and cameras. Along
with minerals, basic commodities and tropical agriculture, these, as we have seen, are precisely the goods apt
to be exported, in ever-increasing abundance over steadily lower tariff walls, by the underdeveloped countries.
For the domestic producers, the future is undoubtedly
bleak. Some large manufacturers may be able to contract and to specialize in newer synthetics, and in lux-
ury items. But the less efficient will surely go to the
wall. For some of them, even the tariff reductions made
at the last round of GATT negotiations were, in the
words of one Rhode Island lace manufacturer, "another
nail in the coffin."

A fourth major category is agriculture. Some somber
predictions have come from Secretary Freeman's office,
but these seem to be based on the hypothesis that there
will be no lowering in agricultural protection. Under
the Mansholt Plan, or some variant, however, many of
this country's producers of cereals, meat, poultry and
dairy products may finally come into their own, earning
through expanding markets the rewards they have long
deserved as the world's most efficient producers. The
cotton growers of Texas and California will certainly

not lose in a lowering of trade barriers; neither will many tobacco growers. Heavy competition in some dairy products and more specialized foodstuffs are to be anticipated from some European countries. And in the long run the large number of American small holders will probably find themselves, at last, forced out of the rural poorhouse.

What emerges from the projections is a mixed bag. In enterprise after enterprise, Americans will have the upper hand in some products, while foreigners prove to have the edge in others. Italian typewriter makers can broaden markets in this country (Olivetti, in fact, has already taken over Underwood), but American firms making electronic computers can do equally nicely in Europe. The Japanese may undersell American companies in cameras, but the domestic firms are apt to sell that much more film. If Hong Kong is a threat to American producers of unfinished cloth and men's clothing, the wider market for its cheaper goods means bonanza for American cotton growers; not to mention Australian wool growers who may buy American appliances.

But however mixed the results, one dominant pattern asserts itself. The domestic enterprises likely to thrive are precisely those that are currently most advanced, that show the highest rates of growth, that have the best productivity indices, that pay the highest wages, that offer the most interesting jobs, that are the most aggressive in developing new methods and new products. The domestic enterprises likely to suffer are precisely those that are the slowest to innovate, that pay the lowest wages, that have the oldest plant and equipment, that are already on the decline. Thus apart from inducing improvements through competition, Atlantic Partnership will act as an important spur in pushing men and capital from declining to growing industries. It will bring to bear pressure for exactly the kind of mobility the economy most needs. The classic pattern of free enterprise, in other words, will be restored; the "invisible hand" will be freed to do its beneficial work.

Undoubtedly some communities, some industries, some workers and many farmers will be injured. But as one cushion they will have Adjustment Assistance from the government (it should be noted, incidentally, that unlike subsidies, which encourage persistence in uneconomic occupations, Adjustment Assistance promotes transition to new enterprises). As a further cushion there is time. At the earliest, tariff cuts under the Administration bill would begin to go into effect only in 1964, and the full effect would be stretched out over five years. (It should also be noted incidentally that the beneficial effects need not be so long delayed; anticipation is the hallmark of economic man, and undoubtedly many firms will be making adjustments before they are absolutely compelled to.)

How widespread the injury will be is a matter of bitter, and crucial, debate. Protectionists generally argue that further lowering of American tariffs will yield extensive loss of jobs, and slowdown of economic activity; to Mr. O. R. Strackbein, Atlantic Partnership presents the "specter of a chronic and stubborn unemployment." The free-trade argument, as put by Professor Peter Kenen of Columbia, is that it is "entirely reasonable to suppose that there will be more jobs created than jobs lost." At least two officials primarily concerned with achieving full employment seem to concur. Secretary of Labor Goldberg has estimated that not more than ninety thousand jobs would be lost as a result of lower tariffs. Under Secretary Willard Wirtz testified to the Boggs subcommittee that:

> We recognize that the only satisfactory way to create new jobs is to create new markets to have new markets for the products and the services which men at work will produce and provide. It is obvious that filling this country's domestic needs, unmet needs, is the largest and most rewarding new market which is available to us, and it is the most promising source of new jobs. But the fact remains that full employment in this country depends on obtain-

ing and expanding our foreign markets. In our view, it is just that simple and it is just that hard.

Most experts would probably agree that tariffs are not the decisive factor in determining volume of employment. A study by the Brookings Institute showed that an import increase of 15 percent would result in a job loss of only .2 percent—and that makes no allowance for the export increase that might be expected under reciprocal treaty terms, and that would certainly create some new jobs. Given that kind of ratio, imports appear almost insignificant compared to other, domestic factors affecting employment levels. As Oscar Gass has pointed out: "To discuss unemployment in the United States with a primary concentration on international trading is to let a very small tail wag a very big dog." The task that the President has described as the most critical domestic task—the task of finding 25,000 new employment opportunities per week over the next few decades—will be much more importantly influenced by such matters as investment, consumer demand and growth. And to all of these government policy bears a crucial relation.

But as a leading Eurocrat once put it, "We are not in business, we are in politics." If there is one thing clear about Atlantic Partnership it is that it frees the hand of government for creative action. The way in which it relieves balance-of-payments pressures has already been described. So has the way in which it spreads out the burden of supporting economic aid, and the costly maintenance of conventional forces. A sharp whittling down of subsidies is, of course, also in prospect. Under the Mansholt scheme, for example, the world market price, paid by the international cartel, would take over from the federal price support system. It is not likely that this country will knit tightly its relations with such efficient shipbuilders and ship operators as the Greeks and Norwegians, and continue forever to support, on dubious grounds of security and at very high rates, a subsidy program for building and operating American ships. And the whittling down of subsidies will relieve the government of a drain that takes a heavy toll, not only of finances, but even more of energies.

In this light, the effects of Atlantic Partnership on inflation must also be regarded. Almost automatically the threat of foreign competition introduces an effective anti-inflationary mechanism into the economy. Mr. T. V. Houser of the Committee for Economic Development has pointed out that "as tariff barriers are reduced, American labor will become more conscious of the fact that it operates in competition with other workers, particularly in industrial countries, and that it cannot push up wages too fast without causing unemployment." By the same token, American companies will become aware of foreign competition, and realize that they cannot push profits up too fast without losing buyers.

For government, the liberating impact of this built-in inflationary check is enormous. If there was a single problem that baffled, taxed and in the end frustrated the leaders of the Eisenhower Administration, it must have been the problem of holding the line against inflation. To that end they scrimped on defense, neglected the cities and short-changed science and education. Still, they failed—and largely because the levers they were working hardly touched wages and profits in the private sector. Their failure, moreover, had at least an indirect effect on the stable growth of the economy. It is fairly clear that the three recessions of the past eight years were more acute and more prolonged than they needed to be, because the Eisenhower Administration was slow in taking counteractive measures. This was not because it was callous or stupid. It was slow to take reflationary action because it was so deeply concerned, and so properly concerned, to head off inflation. Just because it eases the task of fighting rising prices and wages, in other words, Atlantic Partnership augments the government's ability to moderate recession.

What the government ought to do with newly liberated resources and energies is not much in question. Cities, schools, health conditions and the opportunities for further developing natural resources cry out for action. And under Atlantic Partnership they might get it. For the planing away of subsidies, the propulsion of economic laggards into more promising activities, the final closing down of firms and farms that are just hanging on will eventually take most of the steam out of the negative majority. The legislative pass will finally be forced, and the way opened for the wide-ranging domestic program that has been growing more and more necessary since the war. By themselves, the new schools, the improved urban living and working conditions, the more abundant medical facilities and the bigger dams and power grids will be good things to have. Not the least of their advantages, however, is what they will do for the national economy. For inside what are often denounced as mere social welfare projects lie huge reservoirs of demand for all kinds of goods and all kinds of services. It is only through this still untapped demand that the most critical problem—the problem of the 25,000 new jobs per week—is likely to be met. And one way, perhaps the only way, to free that demand is the way of Atlantic Partnership.

Like the Common Market in Europe, in sum, Atlantic Partnership in this country would start small with matters functional, and build cumulatively to grand effects. It fosters a liberal commercial policy that will itself set in motion a flow from the static sectors of the economy toward the advanced frontiers of industry and the services. It opens scope for government to add direction and momentum to the flow. Given time, it will even dissolve the barrier of the negative majority. But will there be time? Can the barrier be turned in the near future?

IV

At first glance the outlook is bleak. Not one of the domestic reforms entailed in Atlantic Partnership—not the drying up of declining enterprise, not the withering away of subsidies, not even effective measures against inflation—can be got by the Congress on its own merits. To wrap these up in tariff reform seems only to sour the dose. Traditionally the tariff has been the most divisive issue in the national history. A tax on tea had at least something to do with the American Revolution. Not slavery but the "tariff of abominations" produced John Calhoun and the bitter states' rights brew of "nullification." Recently, moreover, the protectionist spirit has been on the rise. During the decade 1951-61, American tariffs stood virtually unchanged. During the first ten months of 1961, there were eighteen petitions for tariff increase, as against an average of ten a year from 1957 to 1960. Formidable as that opposition may be, however, the result is far from certain.

Atlantic Partnership raises issues that cut across traditional divisions. In France the Common Market Treaty was put through by the combined efforts of an arch-capitalist, Jean Monnet; an arch-Catholic, Robert

Schuman; and an arch-Socialist and anticlerical, Guy Mollet. In this country a parallel alignment is shaping up. Atlantic Partnership has been plugged by Democrats (John Kennedy) and Republicans (Dwight Eisenhower); by Southerners (Herman Talmadge) and Northerners (Christian Herter); by Eastern opinion (the *New York Times*) and Western opinion (the San Francisco *Chronicle*); by classic liberals (the New York *Post*) and classic conservatives (the *Wall Street Journal*). With some reservations, the American Farm Bureau, the AFL-CIO and the Chamber of Commerce have all recommended it to their clients. And this is no haphazard combination, put together, *ad hoc*, for the occasion. It is the advance guard of a potent but little advertised force —the foreign policy majority.

At its head stands the power of the President—"a world power," as Woodrow Wilson once called the office. In battle against the Congress, it has advantages cited long ago in *The Federalist:* "information; always in session; activity; secrecy; and despatch." In foreign affairs particularly, the office commands unique authority. So strong is the stigma of letting down a national leader in dealings abroad that the Congress even went along with so transparently empty a program as the Eisenhower Doctrine for the Middle East. Indeed, in the postwar years, no major foreign policy initiative taken by the President—however risky, however at odds with local interest—has failed of Congressional support.

Joining with the President in the foreign policy majority is that loose collection of eminent business executives, lawyers, government officials, churchmen and intellectuals sometimes known as the American Establishment. Distinct from European counterparts in being very broad and in lacking invidious motive, the American Establishment is characterized chiefly by an absence of party line; the elite in this country has power but not purpose. Apart from social and old school ties, its typical mode of expression is the panel study, an assemblage of outside experts for the purpose of finding out what to think—the oracle hiring a ventriloquist. But on one issue the American Establishment is militant. Its common denominator—the physical that has to be passed before entry into the club—is commitment to American engagement abroad. The higher posts in the State Department and the security and intelligence community have traditionally been filled by the Establishment. As Richard Rovere has written: "The Establishment has always favored foreign aid. It is, in fact, an issue on which Establishment discipline may be invoked."

Lastly, there is an even less explicit grouping of interests, sections and classes: the foreign affairs public. It includes a wide variety of enterprise with a heavy stake abroad—from Standard of New Jersey to the cotton Senators of Mississippi. The Atlantic, Pacific and Gulf coasts also seem to look abroad. There is impressive evidence that the large white-collar population of the suburbs—perhaps by reason of the conforming instinct—has a bias in the direction of overseas engagement. Some of their Representatives—for example, Thomas Curtis of Webster Groves, outside St. Louis; or Frances Bolton of Lyndhurst, outside Cleveland; not to mention Richard Nixon of Whittier, outside Los Angeles—have been down-the-line internationalists in the Congress. In the 1952 fight for the Republican nomination, the suburban white-collar class was heavily for Eisenhower against Taft. It had been for the internationalist Dewey in 1948, but for Roosevelt in 1944 and 1940. "The white-collar people," the election analyst Louis Harris says flatly, "are highly international."

Ill-defined as this ramshackle jumble of power, influence, interest, tradition and affectation must seem, it has an impressive record of accomplishment. In the postwar era, it has sustained this country's commitment abroad. Time after time, in test after test, it has prevailed—sometimes by a margin so huge as to make the opposition seem nil. It won the day for UN membership; and NATO; and the immensely difficult project of fighting limited war in Korea. It has kept huge sums of foreign aid flowing through three recessions. It beat

back the Bricker Amendment. And in supporting Atlantic Partnership, it disposes of one overpowering
argument.

If Atlantic Partnership is rejected—if the trade bill
fails or, a more likely and therefore more dangerous
prospect, if an inadequate bill emerges—then the hand-
writing is on the wall. The static sector of the American
economy will continue to produce goods and services,
in diminishing demand, at steadily higher prices. The
dynamic sectors will continue to grow, but at a reduced
rate, because markets abroad will be increasingly protected against American goods. Government, more and
more paralyzed by subsidy requirements, obliged to
fight inflation with inadequate tools and still bound by
the negative majority, will be shorn of means to invigo-
rate the economy. At the same time, foreign commitments will be on the rise. Unable to find markets for
their goods, Japan, Latin America and many of the underdeveloped countries in Asia and Africa will beat
more insistently on the door of the American treasury.
The European powers will almost certainly drift off
into a nuclear defense of their own, denying this country any sharing of the security burden, offering for
exploitation by the Communist bloc a split of gigantic
proportions, and virtually foreclosing any chance of
limiting the spread of nuclear weapons. The nation will
thus find itself with a declining base of domestic

strength, and a steadily widening horizon of overseas obligations. Sooner or later the toll will be taken in domestic upheaval or foreign catastrophe—perhaps both. The United States will have to default on power; resign from history.

Set against that grim future there is the alternate possibility of Atlantic Partnership; a partnership in growth, plugging the United States into the dynamism of Western Europe and the Common Market: the Old World called in to redress the balance of the New. It is hard to believe—it is almost inconceivable—that as between a prospect so miserable and another so inspiring the wrong choice will be made by a people that has been so generous, that is so little under the constraint of poverty, ignorance and fear, that has, so much, the future in its bones.

Acknowledgments

This book was written in a brief span, and during that time there was hardly any conversation I did not find relevant, hardly any reading matter I did not find pertinent. Many, many government officials gave generously of their time and insight. Paul W. Douglas and Townsend Hoopes read parts of the manuscript, and provided useful criticism. The library staff at the Council on Foreign Relations was most cooperative in making available research materials. For more technical bibliographical assistance, I am indebted to Albert Wohlstetter of the RAND Corporation for help on military matters, and to William Diebold and Henry Aubrey of the Council on Foreign Relations for help on economic matters. A section, in Chapter 2, on the process of American strategic thought, owes much to a painstaking essay by Morton H. Halperin in the June, 1961, issue of the *Journal of*

121

Conflict Resolution. For style and general outlook I have drawn heavily on the works of the late British historian, Sir Lewis Namier—a great man too little known in this country. John Fischer of Harper & Brothers sustained my spirits all along the way with friendly advice. Genevieve Young performed prodigies to make early publication possible. During the writing of the book, my mother, my brother and my wife bore sad blows with fortitude, and my debt to them is more than I can say.

About the Author

Joseph Kraft was born in New Jersey in 1924 and educated at the Fieldston School in New York, Columbia College (where he was Phi Beta Kappa and Class Valedictorian), Princeton University (where he was a History Fellow) and the Institute for Advanced Study at Princeton. During World War II, he served in the United States Army for three years as a Japanese translator.

Mr. Kraft began writing professionally at the age of 14, as a school sports correspondent for the New York *World Telegram*. For six years he worked on the editorial staffs of the Washington *Post* and the *New York Times*. As a free-lance writer since 1957, he has contributed articles on foreign and domestic politics to many of the major magazines, including *Harper's Magazine, Foreign Affairs,* the *Saturday Evening Post, Esquire,* the *Observer* of London and *l'Express* of Paris.

In 1958, Mr. Kraft won the Overseas Press Club award for Best Magazine Reporting of Foreign Affairs. In 1960, he served as a traveling speech-writer on the Kennedy campaign plane. His first book, *The Struggle for Algeria,* was published by Doubleday in 1961.

Set in Linotype Janson
Format by Sidney Feinberg
Manufactured by The Haddon Craftsmen, Inc.
Published by HARPER & BROTHERS, *New York*